Down Second Avenue

DOWN SECOND AVENUE

Ezekiel Mphahlele

LONDON · BOSTON

First published in 1959
by Faber and Faber Limited
3 Queen Square London WC1N 3AU
First published in this edition 1971
Reprinted 1972 (twice), 1980, 1984, 1985 and 1986

Printed in Great Britain by
Cox & Wyman Ltd., Reading

ISBN 0 571 09716 2

The best lack all conviction, while the worst
Are full of passionate intensity

W. B. YEATS

To

Eva, my late Mother
Grandmother
Aunt Dora
Rebecca
. . . and Jenny who bullied me
into telling her about them

One

THE TRIBE

I have never known why we—my brother, sister and I—were taken to the country when I was five. We went to live with our grandmother—paternal grandmother. My father and mother remained in Pretoria where they both worked, my father a shop messenger in an outfitters' firm; Mother as a domestic servant. That was in the autumn of 1924.

I remember feeling quite lost during the first weeks in that little village of Maupaneng, seventy-five miles out of Pietersburg town; a village of about 5,000 people. My grandmother sat there under a small lemon tree next to the hut, as big as fate, as forbidding as a mountain, stern as a mimosa tree.

She was not the smiling type. When she tried, she succeeded in leering muddily. But then she was not the crying type either: she gave her orders sharp and clear. Like the sound she made when she pounded on the millstone with a lump of iron to make it rough enough for grinding on. I do not remember ever being called gently by her. One of her two daughters was the spit of her; the other anaemic and fawning. But they seldom came home. They worked in Pretoria. When they were not working they had children without being able to secure a man they could really call a husband. I haven't seen them or my grandmother now for the last twenty years, although I know they are still alive.

Things stand out clearly in my mind from those years: my granny, the mountain on the foot of which the village clung like a leech, and the mountain darkness, so solid and dense. And my granny seemed to conspire with the mountain and the dark to frighten us.

My parents bought two goats. I was happy because the animals seemed to understand that we needed their company, my brother and I. Our sister was almost altogether blotted out of the picture. Even now I cannot remember her as she was those days.

We took the two goats out every day and gave them young juicy leaves. It was great fun to feel the tickling sensation in our hands as the creatures nibbled at the leaves; and it was a disappointment when they disdained our offer and ate off the bushes.

The first day I went to school was not a particularly pleasant one. I was bewildered most of the time. We had to walk seven miles to and back.

There we were, a mighty crowd in a large hall, and the old teacher in front of us; an elderly, tired-looking gentleman. I still wonder how he managed us, if he did at all. There we were, chanting away the multiplication tables and word spelling: M-A-T, indicating each letter by clapping of hands. The teacher bellowed out: 'F-O-X, *fokos*; B-O-X, *bokos*; F-I-X, *fikis*,' which we echoed while we marvelled at the look of the words on the board and the miraculous sound of them.

One of the families in the village kept their goat among ours. Their boy and I alternated in herding them and going to school. I began to detest the whole idea of school. I came to associate it with physical pain—with the rod, which the teachers applied liberally as a panacea for teaching and organizational ills. If I had any choice in the matter, I should rather have revelled in the sun, the music of the birds, a plunge into a cool stream than go to school.

Yes, I hated school, and swore to myself I would loathe it to the end of my life. The faces of those pedagogues seemed to tell a story of torture. And they seemed to want to work it off on us with a rod. So I rather enjoyed it whenever I went with my grandmother and paternal uncle to the fields beyond the school and spent a few days ploughing or hoeing or keeping the birds away or harvesting. I ceased to regard school as any place where a sensible person might spend a day. Indeed all other children attended school by fits and starts. And the teachers seemed to view it with nothing but boredom.

The Tribe

'You're not from school today, Eseki, and I can see it in your eyes,' my grandmother said, looking away from the broom she was making out of grass straight into me.

'I'm from there, Granny.'

'Don't lie to me!' She was in the wrong mood. I smelled trouble.

Just then my uncle, who lived with us, came in.

'You were not in school, Eseki, and you'd better not deny,' he said, towering over me like a blue gum tree.

Yes, I hadn't been to school. I had spent the day with friends up in the mountains. I paid dearly for this with a lash.

We had also living with us a young woman, Sarah. She had been adopted by grandmother after her mother died while giving birth. Sarah was always my refuge. She often nodded to me and smiled as though to co-opt me as an ally against this tyranny.

Half a dozen donkeys were added to our livestock. The boy with whom I took turns in looking after the goats and donkeys was quite big; and he wanted to feel that way. So he insisted that I say 'big brother' whenever he called me. If I forgot he gave me a shove or he pinched me. Or I got the stick.

'There's going to be moonlight.'

'And then?'

'Forgotten the river?'

'Oh, the fight, you mean.'

'Yes.'

It was like that. Moonlight, the river fight; with bare fists; where anyone could challenge anyone in the circle who felt for a fight. Then half a dozen or so couples fought it out in the 'ring' formed by the spectators. And we hit away on the white sands of Leshoana in the moonlight.

Some moonlit nights we went out to hunt hares and rock rabbits. It was fun. We came back in the early hours of dawn, our feet wet with dew, our chests heaving with the freshness of morning life. How we laughed when someone happened to be startled by a hooting owl.

Leshoana. A mighty broad river with white sand. Legend had

it those days that a cluster of stars had fallen from grace and were thrown out of the heavens. And on their way down they were changed to sand, white sand. This had heaped up and later washed into Leshoana. Tame when dry but a fierce power, in flood, this river.

On one side of the river were Christian communities living together according to whether they were Methodists, Presbyterians, Dutch Reformists. On the other side there were tribal kraal communities. The Christians called them 'heathens'.

We were often told there were witches among the 'heathens'; and so we were not to walk on their footprints if we knew they had walked there; we were told to hold our breath when we passed them because they smeared witches' fat on their bodies; we were told not to stray among their villages because they were addicted to whipping Christians. But we often went across to look for lost goats or donkeys and they received us warmly, if with aloofness, at their communal fire-places. I never told grandmother that I ate baboon flesh at a kraal one day.

But often, if a Christian chanced to meet a circumcision school, the initiates gave chase and beat him up, swearing at him and all his ancestry in the process. There were certain areas away in the mountains and forests which were regarded as private property and sacred ground for their schools. They felt insulted and outraged if an alien trespassed; they thought we had no right to know the secrets of their creed.

I remember Old Modise say at our village fire-place: 'Let them; what right have we to see other people in their naked selves when we wouldn't be caught with our pants down!' 'And besides,' Old Segone would add, 'we all have our secret little gods, Christians or none.'

Two

LESHOANA SANDS

The communal fire-place. Men and boys of the village met here to talk important things and trifles, away from women and girls. The only time women and girls were allowed to come near was when they brought supper in calabashes. Even then they were the younger set. The man whose wife was ill and maybe had no daughter to cook for him had his food with the others at the fire-place. Other women cooked for his sick wife.

We, the boys, had to bring wood with us from the veld when we came back with our goats, cattle or donkeys. While evening milking went on somebody made a fire for the night. We took turns to make fire early in the morning and in the evenings. The fellow who was too lazy to carry wood just was not allowed to sit with us. He didn't wait to be told to stay away either: and one felt disgraced by having to stay at home with women and girls.

We learned a great deal at the fire-place, even before we were aware of it: history, tradition and custom, code of behaviour, communal responsibility, social living and so on.

'When the Swazis clashed with Bapedi. . . .'

'As things were when we lived under Boer rule. . . .'

'That traitor, Mampuru, who slew King Sekhukhuni . . . Some say he was bribed by the Boers because the king was too stubborn to give away his land—the way Moroka of the Brolong had shamefully done. . . .'

'You boys should feel proud to have a teacher who wants to skin you alive at school. It's like making hard leather soft and tame enough to be used. The more lashes he gives you the more it shows how much he wants you to work. Remember, he's like your father. . . .'

Old Riba was like that. I had a hearty distaste for his small voice and his goatee as he said that. And he liked to repeat his words: not as if he wanted to make sure that we heard him, but rather as though he wanted to listen to the echo of what he must have regarded as his wide words. How I disliked his prophetic airs. I delighted in the gossip that went round the village that he had once jumped into cold river water on a night when a Boer detachment raided his village which they suspected of harbouring Britishers. He was said to have stayed the whole night in the water, with his head out like a water-reed: I delighted in the thought that he must have been a coward.

I still remember clearly how stories were told us at that fire-place. One more thing was to be added to the combination that frightened me—that is, grandmother and the mountain. It was Leshoana river with its white sands.

Old Segone was a great story-teller. He probably spiced things up a bit. 'Thema?' he said, pulling in his snuff at intervals. 'He was a fool, that lad.' He swept the snuff off his palm of his hand after satisfying himself. 'It was spring. You know what it is when plants are full of new life. Ploughing was beginning. You know how the air tickles your nostrils and goes right into the marrow —and then you know you're part of that which dies and yet doesn't die. I must tell you Thema was one of us, from a Christian family: yes, his mother and father were married in church. Trouble began when this lad went to the cities of the white man. The way that boy carried himself made me thank my gods that I never worked for a white man in my life.

' "Did you go to church in the city?" we asked him.

' "Please don't ask me any more about church," the lad said. We were sitting here at this same fire-place. I was sitting where Modise is now, and Thema sat in the place next to Riba there.

' "You know, Father," Thema said, like a man with a heathen devil in him, "Moruti Foster was here, I remember hearing him say Christ died on the cross for us all, and he was our brother. I remember that revival meeting, too." And then Thema turned round and said men were not brothers in the city. The Black man must enter the white man's house through the back door. The Black man does most of the dirty work. When a white man who hasn't gone far in school is given such work he says *I'm not a kaffir!* Black man cleans the streets but mustn't walk freely on the pavement; Black man must build houses for the white man but cannot live in them; Black man cooks the white man's food but eats what is left over. Don't listen to anyone bluff you and say Black and white are brothers.

'And the lad shocked us by saying, "I don't know why Jesus Christ wasted his time teaching mankind!"

' "You read too much," I said to him, "and believe too little."

'We were afraid for Thema's mind. Something seemed to have happened to him in the city. Something terrible and dark. He just wandered about, as if he was waiting for something to happen. It did. It was between him and a girl from Molepo's village, a heathen. They saw each other many times after that. But the girl's brothers were watching him. On a rainy day they got angry. That was when they found Thema and the girl together. He tried to run, but they brought their sticks down on him. He knew that before long Leshoana must overflow and shut him off. That wouldn't do. From a long way off he heard the wailing that you all know, floating all along the river, to warn everybody: *Mantlalela, Mantlalela*—the river is full, the river is full—by the time he reached the river the men had left off beating him. And she was there, waiting for him. She had run faster than him! Let us cross before the river fills up! she said. No, leave me, I cannot cross. I want to sit down, Thema said. You can cross, and you must live. They will kill you if they find you here. And the young man said, It doesn't matter now. It matters, she replied. That put new blood into Thema. She got her hand round him and he felt her strength as he leant almost his whole weight on her. She kept saying, Come, my love, come, my love, as they crossed the river. And the wailing voices swept down to them and passed on, to be picked up by other people below them.

'Round the river bend they saw the angry face of Leshoana as the water hit the outer bank and rose in an ugly wall. Big rocks rolled as though in a death race, thundering as they hit and bounced on their track; trees turned this way and that as though on the broad back of a huge animal. The two people just managed to gain the shore on the other side. With the last effort, he leapt on to the bank; she took a leap but felt something hook her wire ankle bands. It was a stump of a tree, as Thema thought afterwards. The tug of the water wrenched her hand clean off him. Just as a long wailing cry came across the ugly waters of Leshoana, a woman's daughter gave a scream and was covered and carried away. Thema shouted her name. No help.

'We found him lying on his stomach near the slope and brought him home. He told me all about it afterwards. Some say he's still alive, in a village far away, but I do know that he's a little off his head. That is the story of Thema and the pagan girl.'

Looking back to those first thirteen years of my life—as much of it as I can remember—I cannot help thinking that it was time wasted. I had nobody to shape them into a definite pattern. Searching through the confused threads of that pattern a few things keep imposing themselves on my whole judgement. My grandmother; the mountain; the tropical darkness which glow-worms seemed to try in vain to scatter; long black tropical snakes; the brutal Leshoana river carrying on its broad back trees, cattle, boulders; world of torrential rains; the solid shimmering heat beating down on yearning earth; the romantic picture of a woman with a child on her back and an earthen pot on her head, silhouetted against the mirage.

But all in all perhaps I led a life shared by all other country boys. Boys who are aware of only one purpose of living; to be. Often the crops failed us. Mother sent us a few tins of jam and we ate that with corn-meal porridge. Sometimes she sent us sugar which we ate with porridge. Other times we ate roasted flying ants or hairy tree worms or wild spinach with porridge. I can never forget how delicious a dish we had by making porridge out of pumpkin and corn meal. The only time we tasted tea and bread was when our mother came to see us at Christmas. On such occasions many other people in the village came to our home to taste these rare things. If hunting was bad we didn't have meat. About the only time we had goat's meat or beef was when livestock died. A man might have a herd of fifty or more goats, as we had, and not slaughter one in six months. I can never forget the stinking carcasses we feasted on. Often we just ate practically dry boiled corn.

Killing other people's livestock out in the veld was common practice among boys. Many times we caught stray pigs. Then we pushed rags into the mouth to muffle the alarm that only a pig can give. We had delectable rashers. My brother had the habit of catching stray chicks, cutting off their heads and legs, putting them in an old rag and coming home to tell us that he had knocked down birds with a catapult. That catapult was nearly the death of him because grandmother would have strangled him with it if Sarah hadn't saved him.

If we milked a goat in the veld or a goat kicked over a pail of milk grandmother found out that the evening's supply was short. Knowing that a beating was sure to follow, I poured out some milk into a second pail, pissed into it so that it soured and thickened. I then invented the story that two or three goats had been too long in milk and that their kids had grown up.

But we were not the only mischief-makers. A number of *hopane*—dry land alligators—could whip their tails round a goat's legs and suck the last drop of milk.

And there was a man in the village who raided kraals in the early hours of the morning to milk cattle and goats. Villagers had tired of taking him to the chief's council. They merely shook their heads and clicked their tongues in leave-him-to-heaven fashion. Matters came to a head when one or two men discovered that he was not only milking the goats but was riding them for his sexual pleasure. The village outlawed him.

'Go away,' Old Modise said to him. 'Go out of this village to a far-off land that side of Mohlaletse river. Maybe when you've shaken off the dust of this village you'll lead a new life. We will not report the matter to the chief. He's not a Christian, but he'll be very angry. You've done a thing that would make a heathen vomit.'

If my grandmother heard any one of us but mention the name of the banished man she flung the nearest object at him.

'You heathen!' she cursed.

My uncle was a big, tall, bony man of about twenty-three at the time. Although he had moments of kindness and pity, he could be just as ruthless as his mother and his elder sister, Bereta. He enjoyed seeing me panic on the back of a bucking donkey as a learner. He laughed heartily when a donkey deliberately entered a mimosa bush in order to unseat me. He loved to send me to drive baboons out of a mealie-land for the fun of seeing them rain mealie cobs on me.

'If you meet a female baboon on the road,' he used to say, 'and you both stand still to look at each other, it'll tell you to get out of its way.'

'And then?' I'd gasp.

'And then, my frightened boy, you'll fall ill as you've never done before, thin down to a ghost and the last thing you'll see, my frightened little boy, will be a female baboon saying, Get out of my way. That'll be when you die if I'm your uncle and you're my nephew.'

It scared the breath out of me. His broad mouth and laughing eyes told me he would never come to my rescue.

Yet another thing that stamped the nightmare of those years in Pietersburg was vermin. Bugs and lice. My grandmother had very clean habits, like the rest of the villagers who boasted that they were Christians. 'Dirty as a heathen' was a popular phrase. But no one ever thought he could do anything about bugs. Big, flat, grey bugs with miniature contour lines on their backs. They fell from the grass thatching at night for their raid. You heard them fall on the mud floor with a thud. You tossed and turned and scratched your naked body and heard the other sleepers on the floor scratch themselves, as if they were scratching pots, and groan and mumble. If you tried to catch the bug it dropped off at a mere touch. We sprinkled water on the mud floor before spreading our grass mats and other bedding, but it didn't help. In summer we slept out in the yard, which was enclosed by mud walls and had a smooth mud floor. But we couldn't do this too often because snakes were many. In winter the bugs disappeared and in summer they came back with a vengeance. It never occurred to anyone that there might be a vermin killer.

We had one set of clothing put aside for Sundays. On week days we put on our rags and other clothing which were all patches. Mother was a very good dressmaker. She often asked us if we were given the clothing she had made and sent for us. She never knew what happened to it. Many years later mother told us that she found out the clothes had been preserved in a box; because grandmother thought she was indulging us and she, grandmother, wanted us to be tough. When mother did discover this, we had already outgrown the clothes. They were given away. I was compelled to put on rags for a stretch of many weeks until they became a nest of lice. I'd sit out in the veld scraping off the eggs and crushing lice between the nails of my fingers. I gave up trying to wash the rags in river water. Yet I don't remember ever falling ill except for occasional stomach upsets caused by eating prickly pears excessively. The only remedy for a constipated stomach after a feast on pears was a sharpened stick pushed in through the anus and turned round and round. Castor oil and other laxatives were practically unknown for loosening the bowels.

Three

INTO THE SLUMS

When I was about twelve I noticed something that had already begun to take shape in that part of north-eastern Transvaal that fell under the rule of Chief Mphahlele. The young able-bodied men were leaving the villages to seek work in answer to the call of the city. Vaguely I understood that Pretoria was the Mecca. At Christmas-time they came back in dashing clothes: trousers with wide sweeping pipes, shoes with sharp-pointed front; hats with small brims; jackets with fish-tails, trying painfully but in vain to stretch beyond the hips in length; striped ties; belts with iron knobs and spikes worked into the leather; colours ful handkerchiefs dangling boldly out of the trouser pocket. They told us about the glamour of the city life, the money (£3 a month) and the electric lights and trams and motor cars we had never seen before and had no hope of ever seeing until we were big enough to go to Pretoria. They brought gramophones which they said they had played all the way in the train. They said the thing- we saw in Goldstein's general store were for chickens and not eagles compared with those that glittered in Pretoria shop windows. For a long long time they made us believe that there were very small people singing inside the gramophone. They probably believed it themselves. At Christmas-time Jeemee Roe-Jars (Jimmy Rodgers), then in fashion, yodelled plaintively from various parts of the village.

And there was a less glamorous side to all this. Wherever you went—in the fields, at village festivals, at church and every other place where people congregated—you found mostly middle-aged women, old women and old men. The land was not giving out much. The Black man could work only the strip given him by the chief. The chief had no more to give out. The old men at the fire-place complained endlessly that most of their lands had been taken away by the white man. Old Modise pulled mucus through the nostrils and spat out of the mouth as if to clinch the matter: 'Our sons will go out to the city and the chief can't stop them. The cow is too old and it cannot give milk any more. Are we going to beat it for it?' And the old men looked helpless, shaking their heads like that in the glow of the fire.

The non-Christians didn't seem to like change. Their lands turned into patches of sand, but their young men kept on. 'That's the trouble with these Christians,' they said. 'All they can do is go to church and sing and run to the white man to work for him and they've not the brains of a hippo to stay where their ancestors lived and planted them.'

To Christians and non-Christians alike, what the chief couldn't do was impossible. The non-Christians praised him for allowing them to keep to their way of life and the Christians praised him for having built a big school and allowing them to have churches even although he wasn't a Christian.

I never dreamt that I should go back to the city, which I couldn't picture in my mind anyhow. We thrilled at the idea of riding a train, my brother, sister and I, when our mother came in the middle of the year to tell us that she had come to fetch us. Three things stick out in my mind about those few days. The few days when whatever hand it was that drove the train of my life across the trackless wilds suddenly decided to take a capricious turn. First, my grandmother cried. I had only seen her cry at revival services in the Methodist church house. I knew my mother couldn't just come in the middle of the year like that to move a hard-hearted mother-in-law to tears with a kind of domestic joke. Secondly, mother shook off our lousy rags and scrubbed us clean and wrapped us up in brand-new clothes. That couldn't be a joke either. I overheard her say to grandmother: 'I can't change my mind, any more than I can change your son. They're my children and I'm taking them away.' Thirdly, those bright lights we found on Pietersburg station after travelling many miles of dusty road. I heard Jimmy Rodgers yodel. The train arrived. I was too dazed to be happy. Too frightened to ask questions. We found ourselves at Pretoria station the next day. In the midst of a winter's morning we were whisked away by a taxi-cab to Marabastad, a Black location.

That is how a country bumpkin dived into slum life. The springboard was Second Avenue, where my maternal grandmother lived with Aunt Dora and three uncles, all younger than my mother. The eldest uncle was a policeman at Witbank.

After a few days my brother, sister and I went to live with our mother and father at Fifth Avenue. We occupied one room they had hired.

It didn't take long for us to notice that it wasn't all right between our father and mother. They were always quarrelling; especially at week-ends, beginning on Friday evenings. We soon discovered that the main subject of the wrangling was money. Father was not bringing money home. We came to know that was why our mother fetched us from the north. I was thirteen then, my brother three years younger and my sister five years younger.

Mother did dressmaking for an African tailor just outside town. In the evenings she brewed beer out of corn malt to sell. The family's budget was all on her shoulders. She was hard-working and tough. She never complained about hard work. Father walked with a limp as one leg was shorter than the other. It had been broken by a wagon wheel in his teens. But he could cycle fast and he used to bicycle to work. Town was only two and a half miles away. He drank like a sponge, especially home-brewed beer which he had the tendency of commandeering and entertaining his friends with. My mother got very angry but couldn't do anything about it. No pleading could move my father. When he wanted *skokiaan*—brewed with yeast and water—he went to Cape Location, where Coloured people lived, just the other side of the Asiatic Reserve next to us. *Skokiaan* being much stronger than malt beer, my father often said threateningly to my mother: 'I'll go drink skokiaan for you.' But then he was so violent by nature that he didn't really need something to light a fire under him.

We'd never really known Father before. And now living close to him and seeing him at close quarters, I realized that his face was unlikeable. Like his mother, he couldn't laugh heartily. His facial skin clung too close on to the bones. There was something brutal and razor-like about the corners of his mouth; as there was about his limp and the back of his head. He was seldom in a mood to play with us. We kept close to our mother most of the time.

'How long do you want this thing to go on, Moses?'

'What, Eva?'

'Don't pretend you don't know I need money for food. At least you could worry about your children's clothes. Just look at you, drunk as always. What are you standing up for?'

'You don't want to sell me your beer, so?'

'It's there for you if you must drink. But while you're at it, you might think about the bellies of others that want filling.'

My father looked vicious.

'Don't talk to me like that, damn you!' he bellowed. My mother kept quiet. Every gesture of his was menacing, down to the limp. We got used to these quarrels. But we had a sixth companion in the room. Fear.

'I don't want that man here again, hear?' my father said one evening.

'He's your friend and you know he comes to drink.' She told us to go outside as she often did when she saw signs of a storm.

'Don't talk to me like that! Didn't your mother teach you never to answer back to your husband and lord?' we heard him say, through the window.

'You started, Moses.' We looked through the window.

A crashing clap sent my mother down on her knees.

'I'll kill you, I tell you!' He was going to kick her when out of nowhere a hand held him by the scruff of the neck. It was the man from the next room. My father's eyes flickered in the glow of the candle-light. Mother got up and stood in the corner. We went through a restless slumber that night.

'Why does Father do this to you always, Mother?' I ventured to ask one day.

'I don't know, son,' she replied rather curtly.

'I wish Sello's father was my father too.'

'Why?'

'He plays morabaraba with his boys. Father'd never do that.'

'You don't know what you're talking, Eseki. Besides grumbling never takes you anywhere.'

'I'm not grumbling.'

The matter ended. Mother was good at that kind of thing. Probably every trickle of a thought was pain, but grumble she wouldn't.

The tailor for whom she worked went bankrupt. She couldn't get another dressmaking job. Factories were very few and these didn't take in Black labour. So mother started to do white people's washing. She did some sewing at home for people in the location. She made all our clothes—skirts, trousers, jackets, and my sister's frocks and aprons. And I never saw a louse on me again, and she never left my father to go anywhere in dirty clothes.

He, on the other hand, continued to bully, grouse, roar and fume. Mother did a brisk business in selling home-brewed beer. He drank elsewhere and came to her to ask or demand money.

'Don't grumble, Eva!' he'd say when she ventured a comment.

'I'm not going to give you my money if you play the fool with yours, that's what.'

'Let's see if you won't, bitch.'

'You don't need such talk in front of the children.'

'They're mine, anyway.'

'They're mine. What do you do for them?' Her eyes sparkled and I knew from that day that she was going to fight like a tigress to defend her cubs. And from that day I found myself taking sides. I hated my father; his other children no less. Whenever he was in the house we preferred to play outside.

'Eseki, Girlie, Solomon!' We went reluctantly into the room. It was a drunken call. He gathered us in his arms before him.

'I—I—hic—brought you sweets, see? From town—hic.'

My mother was certainly suppressing a laugh.

'See!' He took out a brown packet that smelled of tobacco.

'You give the—hic—others, Eseki, as—hic—the oldest, see!'

This time my mother laughed aloud, as only she could when she was tickled, her big strong arms and shoulders shaking with mirth. She went off into a peal again when my father said, 'Remember, you're my heir, Eseki, and don't let anybody cheat you out of it, see!' His breath smelled of strong beer as he rubbed his rough cheek against mine.

By degrees I drew out of mother the reason why she had fetched us from Maupaneng. He was refusing to maintain us; she had reported him to the Native Commissioner; he advised her to fetch the children—maybe if he lived with us we'd be a constant reminder to him; then she was to report regularly to the Commissioner.

'And those goats and donkeys, *I* bought them,' my mother said. 'He would hear none of it when his mother wrote to him about donkeys she needed for the plough. But don't think any more about it, my son. You're still young and such things are still heavy for your small shoulders.'

Sunday morning. The day when we lounged in the blankets and silently boycotted the early rising custom. The primus stove was purring softly with a steaming pot on. There was an enticing smell of meat, potatoes and curry.

I was thinking of the years at Maupaneng, Pietersburg. The big dark mountains; the fields; my playmates; Old Modise and Old Segone. I could see through the window that it was cloudy outside; and I hated clouds, as I still do today; had always hated them, because they made my soul gloomier than it was, there at Maupaneng and here in Pretoria. In the country it spelt heavy rains. And goats are impossible creatures to manage when it rains. The goats panicked and dashed about madly as if a huge flea had come among them. The donkeys simply would not move in the rain. How often I cried aloud chasing the goats. If I caught one I belaboured the creature with a stick so that it yelled to the heavens for help. I was sure it must understand why I was angry. Afterwards I'd stroke it and mumble how sorry I was. I learned that there is no domestic animal as proud as a goat, as disdainful; it seems never to have heard about flattering the vanity of the human heart.

Running footsteps. I was startled out of my reverie, and so was my brother. My sister followed close behind her, and she tripped over a strip of wood on the threshold and fell—my mother. When he thundered in we knew he had been chasing after my mother. She kept on her knees, clearly hurt.

'I'll show you who I am!' my father said.

'What is it with you, Moses? What are you standing up to do?'

'Get up!'

'I can't—I can't—my knee!'

'This is the day you're going to do what I tell you!' He limped over to the pot on the stove. In no time it was done. My mother screamed with a voice I have never forgotten till this day. Hot gravy and meat and potatoes had got into her blouse and she was trying to shake them down.

He caught hold of her by the blouse and landed the pot in the middle of her skull with a heavy gong sound. She struggled loose from his grip and fled through the door, crying.

Only then did I have the wits to go and ask for help. I came back with Aunt Dora. An ambulance had already been and carried my mother to hospital. The police came and arrested him. We packed our things and went to live with grandmother in Second Avenue.

A few weeks later my mother came out of hospital, bandaged up thickly, to appear in court against my father. I also went to court.

My mother recounted the events of the Sunday morning and all the other things she had against my father before and after. The magistrate sentenced him to fourteen days' imprisonment with the option of a fine of—I forget how much. I remember that he paid it. That was the last time I ever saw my father, that summer of 1932. The strong smell of burning paraffin gas from a stove often reminds me of that Sunday.

Four

WATER TAP

The water trickled down into tin containers. It seemed an age waiting for a four-gallon tin to fill up. More and more people came to wait, the queue got longer, stretching down in snaky fashion. A few of us small boys were also in the queue.

It trickled into a bucket, or a dish, and the queue grew longer, not able to hear itself any more. You could hear a click of the tongue from the many souls waiting there; a click of helpless disgust and impatience. A pilgrimage at a communal water tap. It was like this in Second Avenue, you knew it must be like that at every other communal tap in Marabastad.

Sometimes the people quarrelled, then they laughed, then they eavesdropped and they gossiped. Some sat on their tins. One or two suckled their babies while they waited. The tins filled up at their own good time.

'Tck, tck, so much water in the seas, but none in Marabastad,' said someone. Another tightened her large jaws and clapped her hands and clasped them behind as if to say, 'Wait and despair'. And you knew she had a capacity for waiting.

'You've never heard of such a thing,' said Ma-Janeware, the jet-black woman whose house was the nearest to the tap. 'A tortoise in Ma-Legodi's yard, lying restfully against the wall as if it was laying an egg of mischief.'

'Who saw it?' asked Dokie, the sharp one. She was 'the sharp one' because there was another—Dokie the fat one.

'I'm not going to mention names,' said the Black woman.

'It's not true then,' Dokie the sharp one said.

'Look, it's not my business to be nosing into other people's dark ways, but—don't tell anyone about this. I got it from a goat by the roadside, and you did too if someone asks you. But really Dora whispered it in my ear.'

'How did Dora know it was a tortoise?'

'Who can't tell a tortoise from a stone?'

'A tortoise in town? Nonsense.'

'You're always like that, Dokie. You never believe until you've seen.'

'Oh tell us more, Ma-Janeware.'

'It's witchcraft again. Soon she'll be riding on a baboon down the street at night. That's what you Blacks like best, not so?'

Some women giggled. Ma-Janeware expected it. They always giggled and she always referred to the others as 'you Black people'. Black as soot herself, she claimed to be from Lourenço Marques and widow of a Portuguese trader.

'*Sies*,' my grandmother always said, 'and to think she's as black as Satan's pit!' Ma-Lebona of the house across the street agreed.

I had overheard Aunt Dora tell somebody about our next-door neighbour's dark practices in witchcraft. She swore she had seen a tortoise in Ma-Legodi's yard. 'One of her creatures,' Aunt Dora said.

Time ran out with the same slow, relentless and painful flow of tap water. If you watched the water long enough, it gave the illusion that it was running out faster. But the illusion soon passed. We all waited with dry patience. Often I imagined the Leshoana river running down Second Avenue. With more water than we could ever need. I thought of those abundant springs on the mountain side. Sitting on my tin, I might doze off and dream of the torrents of rain in northern Transvaal. Rains that came down with a fierce purpose and made you so wet that you didn't bother to stop to urinate: you just let off while you walked.

Soon it was quiet in the queue. A man was passing. It was Boeta Lem (Brother Blade), as we boys called him. No one could say what his correct name was. We all knew him as Boeta Lem because he was wont to brandish a long knife when his blood boiled. This Saturday morning the Blade walked with an indifferent, slouching if impudent gait, and with his trousers frayed, exhibiting a long slit from the bottom upward. The torn pipe seemed to sweep the street. He walked with a stoop of bravado. Menacing. He had a handsome face and, if you didn't know him, you might think butter wouldn't melt in his mouth. Yet when Boeta Lem once started to get vulgar, his whole self seemed to curdle, his mouth fumed with foul language: 'You can light a match on his big red eyes,' Old Rametse used to say.

When Boeta Lem was out in the streets, people edged to the sidewalks, such as they were, which meant they almost ran into other people's houses. To make things worse, he went about with a ferocious dog.

'Kill a man made in the image of God,' said my grandmother, 'and you can never wash off the blood.'

He had served a five-year sentence in jail for murder. His neck had come within an inch of hanging, but he got off with culpable homicide.

'You can never stop murder that way,' my granny said. 'They should do what the Boers used to do. Kill the man who has killed another. I don't know, but the Government is a strange person.' And Old Rametse thought one day Boeta Lem would spring upon everybody in Second Avenue. 'That dead man's blood's going to make Boeta Lem so crazy one day he'll let hell fire loose upon us all.'

Boeta Lem lived with an elderly Father and his ferocious dog in a hired room up Second Avenue. Boeta Lem had always worked at night, but nobody seemed to know what kind of work in particular. But somehow he seemed able to maintain his Father and himself in old clothing and his dog in vicious temper.

About midday the water queue got shorter, and at about one the place was clear. It was most annoying to us boys because we missed going to the market to work for a few shillings for bread and *atcha*—mango boiled in 'hot' red curry mixture—during school recess. It also meant that we'd have to collect our pennies and tickeys from boys who owed us—a thing that brought us poor results.

Marabastad, like most locations, was an organized rubble of

tin cans. The streets were straight; but the houses stood cheek by jowl, rusty as ever on the outside, as if they thought they might as well crumble in straight rows if that was to be their fate. Each house, as far as I remember, had a fence of sorts. The wire always hung limp, the standards were always swaying in drunken fashion. A few somewhat pretentious houses could be found here and there. These were, like the rest, of corrugated iron. But they had verandas paved with concrete, and the pillars were of concrete too. The grim old man down our street who worked for the Portuguese Legation had such a house. There was one in Tenth Avenue, and two in Thirteenth Avenue. The other verandas, where any, were paved with mud, and about four poles supported the roof unevenly.

There was only one house which had a flower garden. This faced Barber Street, and it belonged to a man who boasted a Coloured wife, Gertie, and a large brood of uppity children who were good at insulting their father because of his very dark complexion. In fact, this family was reputed to be the only one that had a coal stove. It was possible, because at Christmas-time long queues of Marabastad residents stood waiting with dishes of dough in front of the Indian-owned ABC Bakery, to have bread or cakes baked at a shilling for a standard dish.

In the mornings and afternoons Marabastad was always covered by a blanket of smoke coming from the coal braziers which were put in the yard to burn out before we carried them into the houses in winter, or in the backyard in warm months.

The backyards were always inclined to be dirty, much as the people swept them continually with home-made grass brooms. Most of the houses had a room or two to let out to a family or single persons. So it was not uncommon to find about three braziers blazing away in the same yard.

Ra-Stand,[1] as we called the inevitable white superintendent of the location, was always particular about keeping the streets free of dirty water and dead cats and dogs. But the backyards seemed to be beyond him. The only time we ever saw this personage was

[1] *Ra*—The Sotho word for *Father*.

when we went to pay our fourteen shillings rent or when he drove up the only tarred road, Barber Street; which was the reason why he was thought of only as the owner of Marabastad stands. Otherwise, the location seemed to be the property of the police. Farther into the location, dirty water and flies and dead cats and dogs and children's stools owned the streets.

Marabastad wasn't fenced in as other locations outside Pretoria were. Nor were Bantule or Cape Location. So one could enter it from various directions. But the only white people we ever saw in Marabastad apart from the location superintendent, and the police, were a white minister of the Methodist church or a white priest of the Anglican church and a school inspector who came and went surreptitiously. Many years later a white woman came to put up a soup kitchen. After a few months she disappeared with the kitchen. It never occurred to us that a white person could ever have cause to be in the location unless he was in charge of something or some people. I never even gave it a thought, and I don't think any other resident ever felt concerned about it.

Five

THE LOCATION

We were getting used to Second Avenue life, my brother, sister and I. Avenues and streets were new to us. Now why would people go and build houses all in a straight line? Why would people go to a bucket in a small building to relieve themselves? Why would people want to be cut off from one another by putting up fences? It wasn't so at Maupaneng. Houses didn't stand in any order and we visited one another and could sit round the communal fire and tell one another stories until the cocks crowed. Not in Second Avenue. And yet, although people didn't seem to be interested in one another, they spoke with a subtle unity of voice. They still behaved as a community.

My grandmother was head of a large family. She was a Mopedi, whose father had also been a Mphahlele, but no blood relation of my father's. So many people were surnamed *Mphahlele* that Chief Mphahlele decreed that every one but those of his family should look for a new surname, because, in any case, the name didn't necessarily signify blood relationship. But then several had gone to the cities, and he gave it up. Grandmother had been married to Titus Mogale, a Mopedi of Sekhukhuniland in the Lydenburg district. Both of them were but children when the white 'Filibusters', led by Captain Ritter, were trying to dislodge King Sekhukhuni from his mountains. Grandmother told me how the Bapedi had always hated the Swazis, down to this day, because when the 'Filibusters' had failed to capture the King of the Bapedi, Ritter had organized blood-thirsty Swazis, who subsequently wormed their way through and slaughtered every man, woman and child in the hills and captured the King.

My mother, Aunt Dora and three uncles were born in the

district of eastern Transvaal. Aunt Dora, her three children and the three uncles, lived with us. And we had two rooms. Both were bedrooms and the room which had a table and four chairs was bedroom and sitting-room. We cooked on the back veranda. Granny leased three rooms. My mother, eldest in the family, worked in one of the suburbs as a domestic servant and lived in. She came to see us one Sunday in a fortnight.

Here the young men who migrate to the cities to work still fight as they did on moonlight nights in the country. And so every Sunday afternoon they march with big broad slabs of human flesh they called feet to some place outside the city. They moved in rival teams. In Pretoria these 'Malaita' were provided with a piece of ground and they marched under police guard. In this way, the 'Natives let off steam', as the Pretoria City Council said.

Our house faced Barber Street. It was a family recreation to sit on the veranda on Sunday afternoons. The *malaita* beat on the tar with their large feet past our house; the police dispersed in front of our house before going each to his beat; visiting domestic workers from the suburbs passed our house before they swept into the location, and passed in front of our house again on their way out. It was a common Sunday afternoon spectacle for a policeman to pass in front of our house propelling a man by the scruff of the neck to the police station. Women particularly fascinated us in their various styles of dress. Some hobbled past in awkward high heels, evidently feeling the pinch; others were really smart and enviable.

Our fence needed constant pulling up because it was always falling. Grandmother said how she wanted to plant flowers. We tried valiantly, but none of us had the guts to fetch water for the plants. We gave it up. The best we ever got to doing was set up a grape-vine creeper which made pleasant shade for the family to do washing. The rusty iron gate was a particular nuisance. The ants kept eating up the standards underneath, and we kept digging in the poles until we, the gate and everything else about it resigned ourselves to an acute angle and we piled stones around the standards to maintain the *status quo*. We swept the yard, however, a ten-foot border on all sides of the corrugated walls. The women made a lovely path from the gate to the front door, branching off to the back of the house. This was skirted on either side by small mud walls, and the floor was paved with mud smoothened with a slippery stone and then smeared with dung. Small pebbles had been worked in in repeated triangular patterns. A small wall separated this path from our ash dump, where we constantly scratched for coke to use again in our braziers. The ash we then poured into the garbage can. Towards the front end of our yard, facing Barber Street and Second Avenue, we often planted maize. From this patch we harvested exactly seven cobs most years. We, the smaller members of the family, netted half a cob each. Our backyard was fenced with a four-foot mud wall. The floor of the yard was paved with mud because that was where we cooked—we and the tenants in the two back rooms. These rooms, together with our passage that ran from the back to the front doors, opened on to a small veranda. This we used as a kitchen in the winter. Our kitchen table stood at a corner, for as long as I can remember, where we had found it when we came from Pietersburg. The floor of this porch, not more than six feet deep, was laid in broken uneven slabs of slate. No matter how hard we scrubbed the slabs, there were always spots of candle wax which stuck out like carbuncles.

At another corner Mathebula kept his blankets and the sack on which he slept on a soap box. He slept in the porch. He was a witch doctor and had dropped in one day to ask for shelter. It turned out that he had come from Shanganaland in the north and was homeless. Grandmother had kept him. The ash around the fire-place was a perennial problem. The corrugated iron walls were always sooty, except towards the edge of the porch, where Chipile, the Indian soft-goods hawker often pencilled his invoice. At one end of the backyard Mathebula could be seen any morning sitting on a mat, his bones scattered in front of him while he mumbled magic words in Shangana. All of us, visitors alike, tried, as much as room allowed, to move clear of Mathebula's sphere of influence.

I did most of the domestic work because my sister and brother were still too small. My uncles were considered too big. I woke up at 4.30 in the morning to make fire in a brazier fashioned out of an old lavatory bucket. I washed, made breakfast coffee for the family and tea for grandmother as she did not take coffee. 'That's how I stopped taking coffee,' said grandmother, telling us the story of how when she was a girl, someone hit her with a stone and drew blood from the temple. She had picked up the stone and a witch doctor had treated it with some medicines, but this hadn't helped because since then she was unable to eat beef or drink coffee. They made her so sick.

After morning coffee, which we often had with mealie-meal porridge from the previous night's left-overs, we went to school. Back from school I had to clean the house as Aunt Dora and grandmother did the white people's washing all day. Fire had to be made, meat had to be bought from an Indian butchery in the Asiatic Reserve. We were so many in the family that I had to cook porridge twice in the same big pot. We hardly ever bought more than a pound of mutton in weight. Week-days supper was very simple: just porridge and meat. When there was no money we fried tomatoes. We never ate vegetables except on Sundays. We never had butter except when we had a visitor from Johannesburg. Same with custard. And then I don't remember ever seeing a pound of butter. We bought a tickey's—three pence worth—when we did. On such days we, the children, made a queue to have grandmother smear a sparing layer of butter on one slice only of bread.

At breakfast bread was cut up. The grown-ups were given theirs first in saucers. Then I rationed the remainder in slices and bits of slices. Our youngest uncle, not much older than I, picked his first, which was the greatest quantity. Then I followed, and my brother and then my sister. We ate supper out of the same plate, we children, and meat was dished out in varying sizes and the ritual was repeated. We never sat at table. Only a visitor was treated to such modern innovations.

On Monday mornings, at about four o'clock, I started off for the suburbs to fetch washing for Aunt Dora. Thursday and Friday afternoons I had to take back the washing. If I was lucky enough I borrowed a bicycle from a tenant of ours we called simply 'Oompie'—uncle—when he was not using it on his rounds in the location collecting numbers from gamblers for the Chinaman's fah fee. If I couldn't get the bicycle for the morning or afternoon I carried the bundles on my head and walked—about seven miles' single journey. Like all the other tenants, Oompie sometimes quarrelled with grandmother over tidiness. I was sure, then, that I wasn't going to get the bicycle. When I walked I couldn't use the pair of tennis shoes I'd been bought for Sunday wear. Winter mornings were most trying when the air penetrated the big cracks round the edges of my feet.

When I came back I went to school. I could never do my homework until about ten o'clock at night when I had washed up and everybody else had gone to bed. We all slept in the same room which had boxes of clothing and a kitchen dresser. My aunt and her husband slept in the room which had a table and chairs.

Because we were so many in the family, there was only one bedstead—a three-quarter institution occupied by grandmother and Aunt Dora's children. The wooden floor of the room we slept in had two large holes. There was always a sharp young draught coming up from underneath the floor. Coupled with this our heads were a playground for mice which also did havoc on food and clothing.

Sometimes I stole cooked meat and put it in my pocket. I forgot all about it until I was reminded by a large hole in the pocket where our night visitors had celebrated their jubilee. Early winter mornings a large cold drop of water fell on your cheek or into your ear from the iron roof and you woke up with a start. The only window there was was misty because it had been shut all night. You heard the sharp whistle of the regular steam train passing, from Pietersburg. You heard the coal-black Nyasa police corporal yell his drill commands on the police station premises in First Avenue. You also heard his whistle. Soon, you knew, they'd be marching with heavy booted strides up Barber

Street, past our house. Then they'd stop and disperse to yet another yell, and go each to his own beat on the row of Indian and Chinese shops facing the location. They hardly ever entered the location on their regular beats. If all this happened while you were in bed you knew you were late in getting out of the blankets and the rest of the morning was going to be a headlong rush to the accompaniment of grandmother's mumblings and moanings. You soon learned that it was never wise to leave a window open in Marabastad, even on thick mothy summer nights. We were always scared of burglars and what grandmother called 'wicked night-prowlers who've no respect for creatures made in the image of God'. These were witches. There was also the rain to keep out. Summer and autumn bring heavy rains over Pretoria.

I can never remember Marabastad in the rainy summer months. It always comes back to me with its winters. And then I cannot remember ever feeling warm except when I was at the fire or in the sun.

I was cycling one Monday morning from Waterkloof suburb with a large bundle of washing on the handle-bars. It was such a cold mid-winter morning that I was shivering all over. I had on a very light frayed and torn blazer. Nose, lips, ears, toes and fingers felt like some fat objects detached from the rest of the body, but so much part of me that the cold burnt into my nerve ends.

I came to a circle. Instead of turning to my right I didn't. I couldn't. The handle-bars of the bicycle couldn't turn owing to the pressure of the bundle. From the opposite direction a handful of white boys came cycling towards me. They took their bend, but it was just when my bicycle was heading for the sidewalk of the bend. They were riding abreast. For some reason or other I didn't apply my brakes. Perhaps my mind was preoccupied with the very easy yet not so very easy task of turning the handle-bars. I ran into the first boy in the row, who fell on to the next, and their row was disorganized. The vehicle I was riding went to hit against the curb, and I was down on the ground almost in a split second.

'Bastard!' shouted the boy who had fallen first.

His friends came to me and about three of them each gave me a hard kick on my backside and thighs. And they cursed and cursed and then rode away, leaving me with the cold, the pain, the numbness, and a punctured and bent front wheel.

I picked up the bundle and dragged myself on to the sidewalk and leant against a tree. At first I was too bewildered to think. I started off again and limped six miles home. My aunt and grandmother groused and groused before they had Oompie's vehicle fixed.

'Say it again,' said China from the lower end of Second Avenue. I related the story of my collision again.

'You country sheep!' said Moloi, the boy next door, laughing.

'What d'you think this is—Pietersburg forests,' was Ratau's sarcasm.

It was a joke to all but Ratau. He was a grave-looking boy. Little Links looked indifferent. Even when he said, 'That's the first lesson, you've got to go about town with your eyes open.'

I had stopped worrying over being called *skapie*—sheep—I was told that's the label they stuck on to anybody fresh from the country.

Six

SATURDAY NIGHT

Darkness had set in. Already the street lights were on, and Marabastad location was steeped in a misty light. A few moths were circling playfully round the electric bulbs. It was a Saturday night. Usually Saturday nights are far from dull in slum locations. Everybody is on the alert, particularly the womenfolk.

So it was this Saturday night. An ominous scream pierced into the darkness of the night. I was kicking my legs about for any slight glimpse of a torchlight. I think now how harassing that torchlight was. It was always like this: Saturday night and torch-lights; Saturday night and police whistles; Saturday night and screams; Saturday night and cursing and swearing from the white man's lips. Yet one never seemed to get so used to it that the experience became commonplace and dull from beginning to end. And I was only thirteen.

My aunt was straining the last few pints of beer to pour into a gallon oil tin; and I was keeping watch outside in the yard.

It had to be like this always. 'Go and watch outside, my son'; 'Dig the hole deep, my son'; 'Stamp hard on it, my son'; and so on. The same old cycle. Leave school, my daughter, and work. You cannot sit at home and have other people work for you; stand up and do the white man's washing and sell beer. That's right—that is how a woman does it; look at us, we do not sit and look up to our husbands or fathers to work alone; we have sent our children to school with money from beer selling. . . .

Yes, it had to be thus; always. You are on white man's land; you must do his washing; you must buy his bread with his money; you must live in houses built by him; he must police your area. . . .

The other tins were in their holes already. The last one must be coming through the window soon. She must hurry, or . . . I heard heavy footsteps. Two big men had jumped into the yard, and a big torchlight flashed all over, swallowing up every little object around. Before they turned the corner I had received the tin. In a split second I flung the tin into the next yard. It landed with a splashing thud. I was cursing my fate for the sound but thanking my gods that it had landed in a tank of dirty water, when a white and an African constable came round the corner and focused that terrible blinding light on my face, so that I could only see the big shoulders of the white man on the sides. I became stupid with terror and I trembled.

'What are you doing here, "my jong"?' the big white man asked in Afrikaans. He had switched off his terrible light.

'Nothing.'

'How can you stand here alone and do nothing, Kaffir?'

Silence. Even at this moment I could picture my mother running about to dispose the remains and the utensils.

'What was that I heard when I came in?'

'I was throwing a stone at a dog,' I said. I must keep them here, until my mother would have finished. But I little thought what it was going to cost me.

'Hold the bastard's arms, Jonas, and pin them behind his uss.' The Black constable had hardly reached my hand when the big white hand crashed full on my cheek so that I seemed to hear my name called, and staggered and hit against a pole that was supporting a vine. The Black man pulled me away with a jerk that sent a pain shooting through my side.

'Are you going to tell the truth, "jou donder"?' I didn't care now. Let anything happen, I thought. I got a backhand on the mouth, and in an instant I tasted something salty. While I held my mouth the big white man caught me behind the neck and pressed my face against his other massive hand, so that I began to suffocate.

'Now, this is for your bloody lies, you son of a stinking Kaffir!' With the last word he thrust me away from him. I went down on hard ground.

A big terrible light . . . Shining steel pokers with sharp points for destroying beer containers . . . Heavy footsteps . . . Clanging of steel . . . the sound coming faintly . . . I felt sick. The earth was turning and I seemed to hang precariously on the edge. Everything became dark and black before me. . . .

Marabastad continued to brew beer. Police continued to raid as relentlessly and to destroy. There were Saturday and Sunday mornings when the streets literally flowed with beer. The Chinese and Indian shopkeepers were not prevented from selling corn malt either. Each yard had several holes in which tins of beer were hidden. A house burnt down in Fifth Avenue at one time. When the rubble was being cleared, where there had once been a mud floor, a few holes were found. Dokie, the sharp one, swore that tufts of animal hair had been found in the tins of beer in the holes. 'The things witches can do when they want luck in their beer business!' she said.

Most people feared she was telling the truth. Women brewed some of the most terrifying compounds. 'It's heathen!' grandmother said indignantly. 'My beer's the pure and healthy food a man's stomach needs.' And we never had the fighting type of customer. 'But even with that, God'll help me make money to send my children to college.' By which she meant either high school or teacher-training school. She did send three of her sons to high school and a teacher-training institution.

Interlude

Saturday night. Darkness. Sounds of snoring from my uncle at the corner. Like the muted lowing of a cow. Tomorrow the other uncle sleeping with him on the floor will complain that he had been roused from his sleep by the snoring. My younger brother doesn't stir beside me. Nor the youngest uncle the other side of him under the same blanket as we. They say I'm a bad sleeper and when sleep descends on me there is going to be tugging and tossing and rolling among the three of us. I know the cold air coming through the hole in the flooring boards will whip us out of sleep as it plays upon bare flesh, else one's leg will rest on my neck and then I shall dream that some fiend is slitting my throat and I shall jump up with a scream. My sister also on the floor is kicking the leg of the table she's sleeping under. Grandmother and three of Aunt Dora's children are lying quiet on the old double bed. The only door and the only window are shut. Hot. With two frayed blankets on us it's good to feel hot. I can't sleep I can't get up to walk about in the yard because my bones are aching because I was cleaning the house and turning everything up and choking in the dust I was making. Sweating. Blowing off the salt water from my lips. Kneading my nose to ease the tickling sensation inside it. No use. The boxes and some of Grandmother's worthless collections on the boards resting on the rafters will never be free from dust ever. And then the boxes on the floor containing old handbags and hats and trinkets given by some long-forgotten missus, had to come down from their high stack. But grandmother said to leave them as I found them. Tins of beer dug into the floor behind the stack and the strong smell of fermenting malt and grey spots on the floor around the holes. No policeman will find it easily. Policeman? Saturday night. The men in uniform may even now be sniffing about in the yard. Far to the west end of Marabastad a police whistle, the barking of dogs—no it must be in Fourth Avenue maybe because I hear heavy booted footsteps, it's sure to be a person running away from the law, the police cells, the court and jail. Saturday night and it's ten to ten, I can hear the big curfew bell at the police station peal 'ten to ten, ten to ten, ten to ten' for the Black man to be out of the streets to be at home to be out of the policeman's reach. Year after year every night the sound of the bell floats in the air at ten minutes to ten and the Black man must run home and the Black man must sleep or have a night special permit. The whistle is very near now and the hunted man must be in Second Avenue but the bell goes on peeling lustily and so Black man you must run wherever you are, run. Whistle sound dies away, the bell stops but still I cannot sleep because my back is aching and I am trying to stop my tears of pain so I jump over the others and feel my way to the door opening out on to the ten-foot passage where there is the bucket of water. I take a gulp and go back. Take care not to run your head into the leaning stack of boxes or night will come to an unholy end soon. Music of U-NO-MES band at the Columbia still travels along the night which is what the handbills meant by 'Daybreak Dance'. Still no sleep only things to remember like Saul and Rieta down our Avenue. This morning they woke up to find Rieta had rolled on to their new baby and killed it and they are in the cells this moment. Saul and Rieta. One seldom spoke of Saul without saying Rieta. Drank too much beer, the two, and quarrelled and sometimes Rieta bit one of Saul's fingers and they cried together all which made grandmother say those two were Sodom and Gomorrah and now they went to fetch God's infant from where it had been lying in peace and then killed it. Saul and Rieta, two thin people, thin as Satan's messengers grandmother said, as thin as water-reeds walking for ever as if blown by the wind. The Saturday night buzz has now been muffled. Siki is walking down the street playing his guitar the one he carries about on him, the guitar he plays while he coughs on and on, for he has been coughing ever since I knew him, a long long time. Siki's music comes and goes and comes and goes and

Interlude

I can see him passing on the side of our house, see him as if I were outside, rolling down to the house where he lives with his brother who feeds him and clothes him. Is he with—no, he can't be playing like that if he's with Katrina, Katrina his girl friend who looked after him often. The music fades and fades and is gone fused with the night. 'The white man is strong', funny this comes to me as I seem to hear my mother say it: the white man's strong I don't know you mustn't stand in his way or he'll hurt you, maybe when you're big I don't know you will open your mouth and say what is in your heart but remember now the white man has a strong arm. Saturday night and I'm thinking of school and my classmates. I feel so weak, inferior, ignorant, self-conscious. Saturday night and I'm still thinking and feeling. Tomorrow and the *Malaita* marching through, the women's societies marching through in bright uniforms led by a beautiful and loud brass band who play so that you can hear and a banner floating beating the air. But now it's Saturday and I want sleep. Wonder if that poor man has been caught. Police, police. Mother I fear police grandmother I don't want police Aunt Dora Uncle I fear the police I hate them. Mother says my child when you're grown up when you're big. . . . What's the matter with your herbs? Aunt Dora asks Mathebula the Shangana witch doctor of the family, now sleeping on the back veranda as always. We feed him and give him sleeping room and he gives us strong herbs when we are ill and throws his bones and asks them to tell him why we are so poor and why the police give us no peace and why my uncles and my aunt sometimes quarrel. Mathebula is asleep maybe but I think through his herbs he can see me wide awake. He put a stick into the fire when he went to bed as he always does to keep away other people's baboons but he cannot tell us how to keep the police away. I wonder what the matter is with Mathebula's herbs. . . .

Seven

BACKWARD CHILD

The class teacher said I was backward. The principal said I was backward. My aunt said I was backward. So said everybody. Mother didn't know. I had no choice but to acknowledge it. So when I was placed in Standard Three instead of continuing from Standard Four, it didn't occur to me that they might be wrong.

I found rather big boys, and realized that I was one of the smallest. So I felt consoled. I was in a class of about eighty. In the half-yearly test I took 77th position in our class. Everybody at home shook his head tolerantly and they said they knew how poor country schools were. It was no surprise to them. 'Wonder is you got any position at all,' one of my uncles said.

I scraped through to Standard Four. They called the class teacher by the nickname of 'Kuzwi'. A corrupted form of his real name. A stocky, conservative little tyrant, Kuzwi. He caned at the slightest provocation or whim.

He'd run to ring the morning starting bell when he knew that we were far from the school grounds; just so that we might be late and satisfy what I regarded as something like a neurotic desire to whip. If you were number 50 in a test, and number 51 in a subsequent one, Kuzwi caned you for 'walking backwards', as he put it. If you cycled to town when you might have walked the distance, Kuzwi came upon you with both feet. 'Learn to walk', he said. One day he thrashed me severely. I had come to school with a pair of trousers he had seen torn the previous day. When he asked me who had mended it I said my aunt had. The punishment I got was for not mending the trousers myself. I cried and cried, thinking how unjust he had been. It seemed that

I could never stop sniffing. Every time I thought of the injustice the floodgates of my tears opened.

At recess Kuzwi gave me tea from his flask. I took it but felt ashamed because I wanted to hate him and now his tea was making it difficult at the outset. Kuzwi was a terror in arithmetic. I was too dense to master figures and his ability to work out examples at a terrific speed, coupled with his inevitable cane, did not encourage us the slower ones to do better. I hated the subject more and more and even imagined I hated him. I hated his 'short methods' and his grand display of one 'trick' after another. I hated myself for utter clumsiness with figures. I disliked the way he patted the clever ones on the back.

But for a reason no one could ever explain, this little man was hardest on his niece, Fluenza. She lived with him and it was common talk that he was taking it out on her for what she had done wrong at home. It conjured up a number of dark little stories which fascinated the bigger boys and made us, the cubs, giggle.

'What kind of man is this?' I asked Flu'.

'I don't know.'

'He puzzles me and frightens me.'

'I'm not frightened of him any more.'

'Does your mother know about it?'

'I've no mother, no father.' And she laughed as she said so, with her poignant face that looked as if she would cry any moment.

'Does he beat you as much at home?' Fluenza looked at me with pain in her eyes. I was sorry I had asked. In a sense, I felt that we two were allies, if only passive sponges for tyranny.

The happiest day for us was when we passed out of Kuzwi's hands—to Standard Five. We were going to a thin, pale-faced, coughing teacher who had rusty teeth.

'Moloi! Just look at that!'

'What's it?'

'Those people up there.' I pointed to a high building under construction in Church Street.

Backward Child

'C'mon, Eseki! We're going to be late for bioscope!'

I stood still, amazed at such a structure; it might topple over very soon and crush us under it. I was a little frightened.

'C'mon, you sheep! 'Sthat first time you see a building?' He was impatient.

He was my next door playmate; and he always stood on my side when the other boys threatened to get tough with me. He was full of bouncing spirits and liked to sing aloud at his home so that his voice resounded down the street.

The building seemed as high as any mountain in the northern Transvaal. It conjured pictures of some of these mountains. I had once feared standing at the base of them, lest they flatten me out. But in the city the fear often turned into wonder, although I knew the country fear was sitting quietly somewhere and at any moment the dark creature might begin stalking my tender self.

'Don't you think it'll fall over soon, Moloi?'

'Don't be silly. These white people are clever, chum.'

'But there are some of our people up there, too.'

'It's the white chaps that do all the thinking here.'

'What d'you mean? Up in the north where I come from it's the blacks who do all the work.'

'This is not the north, chum.'

'But blacks are blacks and whites are whites all over.'

'But I am telling you the whites do the thinking here.'

'Like the one that gave me a hot clap at the market this morning?'

'Yes, chum.' Then Moloi laughed till he couldn't sit up any more. He had very large ears and they were the very expression of the gaiety in this boy. I pushed the four-wheeled cart very hard and then jumped on to the edge while it rolled down-street.

I found myself laughing aloud. That was a stinging slap I had got from the large palm of the 'Market Master'. He wasn't the Market Master in fact. He was a caretaker or something like that; but we called him Market Master. He was huge enough to symbolize the man who to us controlled such a big place as the city market.

We had been picking up stray carrots, over-ripe tomatoes and so on to eat in between drives to the suburbs. The 'Market Master' swooped down on us. By the time I saw the white dust-coat flapping next to me, he had struck out with his big paw and the blow at the back of my head sent me sprawling on all fours. A whip cracked on another boy somewhere ahead of me. We scattered. Moloi had loaded our cart with a white customer's vegetables and we set off for the suburbs.

All the way to Sunnyside in the morning I was confused. I wondered whether this was the sort of life one was to continue to live until one's death. . . .

After laughing, as the cart glided nicely on good tarred road, I felt both hungry and depressed. And somehow I seemed to be travelling along a long, long winding road that promised no destination; just like those red roads of my earlier years, where the dust far ahead of you told you the end was not yet. Was it to be thus in the city?

Soon, however, we forgot our hunger, weariness, everything else, lost in the exciting moments of the movies. We always had a large bill for fourpence. Often they showed four pictures and a serial chapter on one programme. Those were the days of silent films: the days of Hoot Gibson, Tom Tyler, Frankie Darro, Buck Jones, Tex Maynard, Tim McCoy; the days of funny actors like Harold Lloyd, Richard Talmadge, Larry Simon, Charlie Chaplin, Buster Keaton and a host of others.

We stood on chairs to cheer our screen heroes. A piano played a medley of noisy tunes which, however, made superb background music. The other boys relied on me to read the dialogue and titles on the screen aloud so that they might all follow the story. I felt really big and important and useful because I could read fast—as fast as the slow tempo of life in those years made it necessary.

'But how do you read so fast?' Moloi would ask me.

'Just like that,' I would answer, smiling mysteriously.

'No use asking you anything,' he would say, genuinely disgusted.

The truth of it was that I used to pick up any piece of printed paper to read, whatever it was. It became a mania with me. I couldn't let printed matter pass. I felt inferior to most of my class at school. I was pretty poor in English, which was the medium of instruction. I read, and read, till it hurt. But I also got a good deal of pleasure out of it. And I felt proud because I was overcoming my backwardness.

Often I didn't have money for the movies. Then one of the boys would pay for me, just so that I should read for them. I managed to be heard above all the din from the audience accompanied by the klonk-onk from the piano, which was constantly playing during the performance.

Eight

THE FOXES

A bunch of us Second Avenue boys were standing about on the stoep of Abdool's shop: the usual after-school meeting-place of the Foxes, as we called ourselves.

'Have you done Kuzwi's sums?' China asked.

He was the one with high cheek-bones and a tight skin over his face, like an Oriental's.

'Let Kuzwi go feed the chickens!' someone said.

'He'll skin you alive, he'll give you such a barking-up, you'll fancy someone's calling your name,' Moloi said.

'You're afraid of him!' China challenged.

'Who isn't?' Moloi said. 'He wasn't happy till he peeled off a boy's skin this morning.'

'That's nothing,' little Links squeaked as if from nowhere. 'You should've seen Kuzwi the day Pongose was on the bench under his cane! That was the day Pongose's trouser seat flew up. A whole patch.'

'And the day Danie wet his pants,' another added. We laughed heartily, and little Links's body looked too frail for so much rocking laughter.

'Remember, boys, Big Eyes dancing with Frans at the Columbia?' someone said.

'Mean when he was dressed up as a woman to trap the big boys?' We bawled out in laughter.

'Big Eyes' was what we called our big-eyed headmaster. He was champion of whipping, and we boys often had the embarrassed fun of holding girls by the legs and arms down on a bench for Big Eyes's caning pleasure. To say nothing of the delight we experienced when we talked about the colour of a girl's knickers at playtime.

Boys in the upper classes often said Big Eyes's caning was patting compared with his predecessor's. We heard stories often of how that gentleman used to buy sixpence worth of firewood, put it on the floor, and order a boy to lie on it for caning. It was crude firewood with splinters and knobs sticking out, so that if the boy tried to move because of pain, the wood pricked him to a more or less stationary posture. The boys used to say Abraham must have laid Isaac on the firewood in the same fashion; so it was a common saying at school that a boy had 'got the Isaac'.

'Oh, I hate that man,' I said, 'and arithmetic too,' reminding the boys of Kuzwi. Old memories were rankling. Old Rametse of Second Avenue used to say that he couldn't see why small boys failed to get arithmetic sums right. 'If I'm told to put three match-sticks in a box, take out two sticks and throw them away, why can't I tell the teacher tomorrow what remains if he tells me today?' he would say.

The three Chinese shops along Barber Street were poor corrugated-iron structures, including that of the rich Fung Prak opposite us. These were purely grocery shops, and they were untidy. The five Indian shops were bigger buildings, of brick. They were tidy, and each shop had grocery and drapery departments. On the verandas of all the shops was a carpet of monkey-nut shells. Abdool's was one of these five. One large window displayed bananas, oranges, granadillas, *kujavas*—as we called guavas. The other window displayed dust-covered articles of crockery and paper masks and tiny toys.

There always lingered in the shop a delightful spicy smell. A door led to the back quarters and coal-yard. On the walls were strewn pictures showing Indian girls in dance poses: sleek, pink and yellow girls with chubby faces and large eyes. There was a legend on each picture in some Indian and Arabic characters. From the ceiling, converging on a central electric cable, hung multi-coloured paper streamers. Once a set was hung up at Christmas-time, it kept up there for many months. Like the paper flowers we bought in a paper-wrapped tin at Christmas and kept on the table almost until the next Christmas after repeated dusting with a rag. I don't know if Abdool ever took the same trouble about his streamers.

At night, with the ten to ten alarm, Abdool called his servants out—a sooty bunch who always looked hungry and non-committal—to bolt up the windows with wooden shutters and iron bars.

Some of us were sitting on the step in front of the door of Abdool's bedroom. Others stood against the wall on either side of the door, like me. It happened in the middle of a guffaw. Little Links and China had the worst of the shower of urine that Abdool's wife threw out of a large family-sized cream-coloured bed pan. It sent us scattering noisily over the stoep, while the Indian woman stood at the door cursing blue fire in the most obscene language. All the while she kept adjusting her *sari*. I noticed how round her stomach was. I remembered that I had hardly ever seen her stomach small, and also I remember overhearing grandmother say to Aunt Dora that Abdool's wife was always expecting a baby.

Poor Links and China went to the nearest street tap to wash. The Indian woman shot out a string of reddish yellow saliva and disappeared. While my mates babbled I stood and watched the saliva mix with the urine on the stoep.

'I wish she dies,' said little Links when he came back.

At this moment we found ourselves gazing at a girl passing up the street. She had a sprightly gait, with arms swinging as if she might fly at any moment.

'Who's she?' Moloi asked with a curious twinkle in his eye.

'The new girl who moved into our street with her father yesterday, stupid,' China said, as if the whole of Second Avenue were expected to be in a fever simply because a new-comer had arrived. The girl was soon swallowed by Moosa's shop next door. 'A fine cheek she has,' blurted Moloi.

'Why?' I asked.

'She comes to this place yesterday and doesn't even ask where's the shop or where's the school or where's the police station!' He spat before the last two words dropped out.

'Perhaps one of those girls from the Rand,' was grave-looking Ratau's verdict.

'What does she think we're made of?' was Khabi's remark.

'My father says nobody asks anybody anything on the Rand,' little Links said.

'Funny place,' China summed up in a detached manner, preoccupied with erasing the itch behind his ears where urine had been.

'Tell you what, Foxes, if she asks you anything, look away, just as if you didn't see her,' Moloi proposed. 'Agreed?' There was a chorus of 'Yes'.

She passed again, and there was dead silence. Only a shuffling of feet and hissing. She walked comfortably down Barber Street and disappeared round the bend down Second Avenue.

'What a cheeky head!' I thought. I thought I saw a look of hurt on the others' faces, but I wasn't sure.

Just then I remembered that I should be getting home. As it was I had overstayed my time. I was not entitled to it, but then the grown-ups had gone to Johannesburg and there would be some freedom in the house. We dispersed. Still, I'd have to clean the floors, dust the furniture before I did anything else at home. Grandmother and Aunt Dora did the white people's washing and never had the time to clean the house. After I had finished, it would be time to go to the Indian butcher and to make fire in the brazier, wash the two pots we had used the previous night, the porridge pot having soaked well by then.

There were almost always tubs of dirty water to carry to the drain at the street tap. The municipality was not strict about dirty water being thrown out on the street. But grandmother insisted religiously that we take it to the drain. 'Otherwise we shall all wake up in the morning to find our hands withered,' she always said. Grandma explained that witches had a habit of taking such water to work black magic with in order to inflict someone they hated with corrosive disease. It was out of the same religious habit that she insisted we should never to go sleep without first putting a drumful of fresh water inside the house. 'What should we do if someone in the house fainted at night?' she argued.

Nine

HAWKER'S DAUGHTER

She had come. And she and her father were very much with us. The two had occupied a house lower down Second Avenue.

'They say he's a very rich man,' said Ma-Lebona to grandmother. She always came in from the house opposite us whenever she thought she had something startling to tell. 'And yet he doesn't look so, God knows, Hibila.'

'You always notice these things, don't you?' said grandmother with a smile. And Ma-Lebona would laugh, rocking all over, with her back straight and clapping her lean stringy hands on her laps.

'You're pulling my leg again, you wicked woman,' Ma-Lebona said. 'Truth to tell, he has a lovely daughter. But I went to greet them and I looked at her face and said to myself by my Father Elisha and my Mother Rabeka who are sleeping quietly in their graves—bless their souls—in the Free State, this looks a cunning cat that can scratch you and draw blood, I don't know.'

'Ach?'

'I say to her father we are happy to see them and we hope they'll also be happy in our peaceful street. And you know what, Hibila?'

'U-huh?'

'The little girl—I think they call her Rebone—yes, Rebone—just looks me straight in the face, Hibila, straight in the face you hear me, as if she was going to say if you dare touch my father I'll scratch your eyes out!'

'You wouldn't touch him, would you?' Aunt Dora asked.

'Go on, Dora, what would the spirit of my Joas say if he saw me—poor man—and he dead only four years now!'

'Will you tell us you're too old to think of Dinku Dikae?'

'Hi-hi-hi-h-i-i! Listen to your daughter, Hibila. She's always wanting to laugh at me. Hi-hi-hi-i-i-i!'

After Ma-Lebona had left grandmother remarked: 'That woman! One day we shall hear greater things from her lips, or a donkey will give birth to a pig.'

'But we have, Ma,' said my aunt. 'Remember the day—go to the shop for coffee, Eseki.' I knew I was redundant audience.

Rebone's father, Dinku Dikae (both names were always mentioned because they make a convenient sentence: Where are the sheep?) must have been about forty when they came to Second Avenue. She was our age, thirteen or so. He was strongly built, with broad shoulders and a blacksmith's arm. His voice always reminded me of the echoes in the mountains of Maupaneng: at once sharp, cold, forbidding and reassuring.

There was such a marked difference between father and daughter. Yet I always felt this cat-like wisp of a girl had the same fire in her as Dinku Dikae. The house in which they came to live had belonged to a woman who had left it after being the lone occupant as long as I could remember. Rumour had it that it had been bought from her. Later Rebone confirmed it to me.

In a short time they had acquired a trolley-cart for which a shed was put up on the roomy side of the yard. Dinku Dikae started a vegetable and fruit-hawking business. Rebone joined us in Standard Five at school. We got to know her well, and she was not too shy to want to make new companions. In fact, everyone at school rather thought she had the unusual gift of drawing friends to herself without crawling on her belly to make them. Some of the girls in the class showed obvious jealousy. But Rebone gave out a tacit challenge. Some bowed under her silent will and charm; others competed for her attentions and favour. It was immediately rumoured that she came from the Reef. It turned out later that she had.

Rebone had big dark eyes which looked as if they were going to jump out any moment. I often imagined I could take them out and play marbles with them. And then her waist made me think of a wasp. Ma-Lebona often snorted, half-humorously and half-impatient: 'That little wasp. God knows Hibila the day she goes ving, ving, ving over our heads, beware! My blood tells me something.'

Rebone did sting one day. But of that, later.

One afternoon we were all feeling drowsy and heavy in class because of the midsummer heat. I wrote a short note: *I love you—Eseki*, which I gave to someone behind me to pass it over to Rebone two rows behind me. I waited drowsily for a reply, not expecting it, really. We were copying history notes from the blackboard, one of the drudges I loathed. I had come to the name of Sekhukhuni. As another piece of diversion, I rewrote the name several times, so that it was finally almost a black patch on the white page of my exercise book. I was thinking, 'Sekhukhuni, Sekhukhuni, if you hadn't fought back against the Boers—you *would* do such a crazy thing, the Boers are so painful—' when a biting clap caught me full behind the ear. I fancied I heard my name called. The classmates who saw it happen laughed and giggled. When I looked back Rebone was reseating herself in her place. An angry hiss like a snake's—such as only African girls can make—came from her pouting lips when our eyes met.

'What's that at the back?' The teacher raised his head which had been bowing to the majesty of summer heat. His eyes looked like a sad dog's. Like a dog he slumped back to his former comfortable posture. My eyes were moist from the pain. But I finished those miles and miles of notes with a new spurt of energy.

In a few weeks' time it had become a habit for me to carry Rebone's books for her when we went home. She told a gaping and bewildered lad much about Johannesburg, which we commonly spoke of as 'Ranteng'—the Rand.

Ten

MA-LEBONA

'She's there!' When Africans say a person 'is there', they mean you cannot but feel she is alive; she allows you no room to forget she was born and is alive in flesh and spirit.

'A mother-in-law has great duties to perform and great ideas to live for,' the woman used to say. I remember Ma-Lebona, about fifty, thin, spectre-like; her chest curving in a little; her whole physical make-up seeming to consist of taut strings which would one day snap and bring chaos and hell fire upon the whole township. I remember her always in her shawl, taking long, lounging strides from one house to another in Second Avenue, thrusting advice down the throats of men and wives. She behaved and spoke as if she were the only person God deemed fit to fashion after the pattern of the true mother-in-law.

When she looked at you, her eyes seemed to wander over the areas of your body first, and then to focus on your eyes. One of her greatest boasts was that she always looked at a person—black or white—in the face after sizing him up. Now African women dare not look men in the face, let alone size them up. Women of her age regarded this as a special quality of boldness in Ma-Lebona.

'A good wife must be obedient to her mother-in-law, she must be able to wash, clean, cook, clean the house and look after her children well,' she always said. 'But the young girls we have today for daughters-in-law, Phoh! They are thick-headed and stubborn.'

If anyone among her listeners did not agree, she told the others after Ma-Lebona had left, 'Ha, you can't teach that woman anything.' Then they would nod their heads in agreement.

'Whatever did Salome's son see in that girl when he married her?' she would say to grandmother. 'I've just been to see them —just to know the *makoti*—daughter-in-law—better.'

'Meaning?' grandmother asked, after spitting on the white man's collar she was washing.

'I mean she's so lazy. A young woman should go out and work or she must do washing to help her husband earn money. She cannot even cook!'

'Ever seen a modern girl able to cook?' grandmother said, spitting with gusto because this was her subject. 'We were taught to cook by the Boers—and Boers could cook, I don't know if they still can.'

'Young mothers should take their children out more often,' Ma-Lebona would say. 'In my day I used to take Joel to the tennis. There he waited in a small cart while I played tennis—this way and that.' Ma-Lebona often tickled grandmother and Aunt Dora by waving her hands left and right alternately, as a two-handed player might do.

'Liar!' grandmother would say, spitting the word into the soap suds when Ma-Lebona had gone.

'But Ma,' Aunt Dora would say, 'doesn't Ma-Lebona's Joel look stupid? I don't know maybe it's the shadow of tennis netting on his brain.'

When she talked tennis, Ma-Lebona often spoke English—as much as she could remember of it: to the total dislike and contempt of many older folk. Nor did she ever forget to mention that she had once been a schoolmistress, trained at Kilnerton Institute, eight miles out of town. 'When I was a schoolmistress . . .' she often began. Which was enough to make the other women feel at once jealous, envious, annoyed and humble. If Ma-Lebona did anything good, it was because she had been a schoolmistress; if she solved any problem or she did not join her friends in any mischievous venture, it was because she had been a schoolmistress; if she did anything she was lucky to be able to acknowledge as bad, she was thankful that she did nothing worse, because she had been a schoolmistress.

Ma-Lebona

Ma-Lebona had been married twice, I heard Aunt Dora tell a friend. The first husband lived with her three years and then 'the bell rang for stopping work', as Africans say when relations are severed, and he disappeared. 'You see, be good to a man,' Ma-Lebona said, referring to a forsaken lover in Second Avenue, 'as I was to my first man—do everything for him, give him good food, mend his clothes, tell him how to keep clean and keep him clean, give him all the comfort, and he leaves you—like my first man.'

The second husband stayed two years with her. Two years of nagging, spying, prying, of scandal. He was very sorry for having given her a daughter, Aunt Dora believed. 'He'd rather have left nothing on earth that would constantly remind him of Ma-Lebona.

The third man in her life did not marry her in church and at the Native Commissioner's. 'They simply lived together', is the African's way of putting it, as if marriage by civil law were like scaling a slippery wall. A son, Joel by name, was born of this union, which lasted ten years.

Trouble came when the woman said to her man one day: 'Old man, you have the money and I have the brain.' Her man raised his eyebrows and prepared himself, Aunt Dora continued. 'We can go and buy an old tram body—you know those the city council threw away at Veldskoen—and we can paint it well, and put up a coffee-house hereabouts.' After her man had thought it over, his only reply was that he had no money, at any rate for such mad schemes.

'Ma-Lebona hammered the point,' Aunt Dora related, 'and kept a rough twig between the husband's buttocks long enough to drive him mad and out of the house. He wasn't seen at Marabastad again after that.'

Ma-Lebona had walked the length of Second Avenue many times, saying, 'Men are stupid, you know, the ancestors help me that I should have seen anything wonderful in their thick heads!'

'That the man should have been reared by that woman for ten years,' some men had said.

'And to think that when he came under her arm-pit we spat on our hands and pointed into the heavens, swearing that if he stayed five years with her, a crocodile would give birth to a buck!' others had said.

Aunt Dora went on to tell the story of Ma-Lebona. Ma-Lebona went into the business of running daughters-in-law.

Ma-Lebona's daughter was twenty-two or so. Like her younger half-brother, she couldn't go any higher at school than Standard Eight which they both failed to pass. 'Their mother is simply disappointed in them,' grandmother said to her friends.

'I have *two* children at Kilnerton High School,' Ma-Lebona used to say to her neighbours, indicating it with two long fingers. 'Some foolish people think it is easy to get children through high school. You have to work, work, work, and stinge yourself rice and stew, and wear rough German print. I do not know what I shall do when they go to Fort Hare!' Fort Hare was in the Cape Province, and was the one and only non-white University College in South Africa; there one might take a degree in arts, science, economics and a teacher's diploma. The woman sighed, gave a despairing clap of the hands and let her arms hang limp. Grandmother would nod as Ma-Lebona said this, inwardly pleased because she herself had sent a son to Grace Dieu teacher-training school in Pietersburg. 'Of course they don't know what it's like, Ma-Lebona. And then their children stand about shop stoeps like a dog that doesn't know where to face when it's going to lie down.

'Like that Boeta Lem letting his hands rot in his pockets like that,' Ma-Lebona summed up, waving her hand in a contemptuous gesture and bringing it back to rest on her hip to clinch the matter.

'The day those children go to Fort Hare,' Old Rametse said, 'the spirits help me never to meet Ma-Lebona!'

Everyone knew that Nkati, Ma-Lebona's daughter, and Joel, her son, had grown up under strict discipline. But while Joel was humble and subservient, Nkati was regarded as a rebellious little upstart who always had an answer ready on her precocious tongue.

'And now she wants to rear daughters-in-law and brothers-in-law,' Aunt Dora said to her friend from Fifth Avenue. 'Comes a suitor and Ma-Lebona wants to keep on the young man as if she wanted to chisel him to proper shape. Now that young man courting Nkati is a fine boy. He told me himself, he says he doesn't like the old woman gazing at him like a cow.'

'What does the girl say about it all?' the friend asked.

' "It won't be long before we leave this house for good," she keeps saying. He tells me Ma-Lebona has said to her daughter: "Your young man is too quiet for my liking. Such men can't be trusted. He will sit there as quiet as a mountain and say very little." To him she said: "I could never sit quiet like you, you know. When I was your age, I used to keep people listening attentively for hours." '

The two young people married. They left for their own two-roomed quarters in Fourteenth Avenue.

'I have asked them many times to live with me,' Ma-Lebona said to grandmother one day. 'After all, the young man didn't pick up Nkati rooting for garbage in Indian backyards. But the couple are just hippo-headed. Jehova of Israel, the boy—what's he but a mere boy—has the pluck to tell his wife he couldn't think of being run by his mother-in-law.'

'And she?' grandmother wanted to know.

'She reckons she belongs to someone else now—so she says to me—and the little heathen actually says "It's not like being married to one's own brother " You know, Hibila, as old as I'm getting now, Black mothers and fathers don't make the same daughters as in the old days—when I was a girl. Those days we were told—not asked—told that the first baby must be born at your mother's. But no, not Nkati and her man. *They* wouldn't do that!'

She kept reminding Nkati, whenever they met, that her man had no respect for old age and had talked to her as no young man, or even old man, had ever done. 'Just like her father, this girl Nkati,' Ma-Lebona said. 'But as sure as the sun's riding high the wrath of the ancestors will break upon them one day.'

I don't know if ever it did. What I do know is that about eight out of every ten educated Africans, most of whom are also professed Christians, still believe firmly in the spirits of their ancestors. We don't speak to one another about it among the educated. But when we seek moral guidance and inspiration and hope, somewhere in the recesses of our being, we grope around for some link with those spirits.

We often went to sleep at Ma-Lebona's, opposite our house, when grandmother and the other adult members of the family were going to be away for a few days. During this time I came to realize how Joel, Ma-Lebona's son, worshipped his mother. Even as a boy, I became embarrassed for him when he fawned like a tame puppy to his mother. It was always 'Yes, Ma', 'I will, Ma', 'All right, Ma' with him. When she was in a temper he was quick to ask her what had upset her, and coax her into good temper. He married the woman of her choice—her old friend's daughter.

'No, child, that stove is not clean . . .'; 'No, child, you must not sit like that when you're in a family way . . .'; 'No, child, one does not cook cabbage in so much water . . .'; 'Your wash-towels need boiling . . .'; 'Joel likes his egg boiled, not fried . . .'; 'Joel does not drink tea, he drinks water with milk in, and both the water and the milk must not be hot. . . .'

The only time I tasted tea with sufficient milk in it was at Ma-Lebona's, and, of course, when I had gone to see my mother in the suburbs.

And so the orders were given. Ma-Lebona was as clean as a cat in a white man's house. So was my grandmother. 'They think they're white people', is a common saying among my folk. Like 'he wants to eat and dress like a white man', or 'he speaks to me as if he were a white man', or 'even if he were a white man I wouldn't carry out his orders', or 'fancy, does he think he's a white man!' Ma-Lebona was simply obsessed with cleanliness. None of the three rooms she occupied (she had a six-roomed tin shack) or the stoep was to be left dirty too long in the morning. She often had meat taken out of boiling water to be rewashed. She kept an eagle-eye over all the household duties. Anna, Joel's wife, obeyed without question, just as all new wives are instructed to do by their aunts and uncles on the wedding day.

'Anna's breaking,' Aunt Dora told the family. Like one who had been expecting it a long time. 'I went to borrow sugar and there was dusty talk between her and Ma-Lebona. You mustn't quarrel with mother, Anna, that Joel with a sheep's skull kept saying. That Anna is terribly lonely, I don't know—remember when she was expecting this baby they have now, Ma-Lebona had so many orders what herbs the poor girl should use and Anna so young she seemed lost.'

'Fitting too, I should say,' grandmother said, picking her teeth and breaking wind in-between times, spitting into her handkerchief which was a large piece off what had once been a napkin. 'I hate witches who walk naked at night. You see your friends smile when you're in luck but you don't know how wicked they may be. No sooner does a new life shoot out and some friend wants to kill it. Friend, friend, friend! Don't think all people like to see you expecting a child. And babies aren't to be had for any sum of money. My mother used herbs on me and I used herbs on all of you and you must do the same on your little lambs. God has given the Black doctor wisdom which the white man hasn't got.'

Ma-Lebona's domestic troubles became a public scandal. She talked freely to neighbours about her daughter-in-law's negligence, loss of respect and many other lapses. When Anna heard this she told Joel, if only so that he knew. She told Aunt Dora of it, all tears.

'She has done it!' Aunt Dora declared, again like one who has been watching out for a cosmic sign of things to come.

'Who?' Dokie the sharp one asked.

'Anna. She has slapped her mother-in-law on the cheek.'

Everybody down Second Avenue was shocked. Tongues were let loose. Some nodded their heads and said, 'It is good for Ma-Lebona. She's met her match.'

'Wicked!' Old Rametse gasped.

'You just wait,' put in others, 'just you wait. The day will come when the truth will out. God moves like a crab—very strange.'

Anna did it again one day. When Joel came back from work, so a gossip told us, he was beside himself with rage on hearing the news from the same gossip. The informer ended by saying, 'That poor man has married a hundred fires put together. That's the way of town-bred girls.'

'She's left,' Aunt Dora announced. 'She told me herself when she left, I have done all a human being can do in this kind of life. And she told Joel he'd never keep a wife because she must also be his mother's wife, and if her mother could help it, she would bear his children for him—Joel.'

'That girl's a heathen!' grandmother summed up.

'That's what Joel called her—and a monster too, and Anna said to me, Sies Dora, she said, this woman has done more than her son to get me.'

We all looked forward to Joel's next wedding. With Kuku, a pretty woman. 'Another from Ma-Lebona's beehive,' grandmother said.

The bells rang. The church filled up. Eleven o'clock struck, the time set for the start. A cluster of girls were talking about the trousseau, leaning on one another's shoulder as if to spy on events. The minister was waiting. The groom arrived. There was a breathless expectancy in the air.

Her car must be late . . . A shoe must be missing . . . Some pins are probably being looked for . . . She may be unwell and waiting for a nurse . . . Oh well, a wedding without some hitch is no good omen for a happy married life, is it? . . . So people whispered. Eleven thirty, eleven forty-five . . . A loud murmur was heard at the door. A shattering hiss ran through the rows of people. Even the minister was fretting. A hum, and the bride seemed to be coming. We craned our necks to look out every time. Increasing whispers.

Pretty Kuku never came.

A car with 'T.J.' number plates—from Johannesburg—had picked her up at the house, people said.

'Girls and boys alike go like bullets to the city of gold—never to return. They've to be picked up, if anyone is interested,' was my grandmother's verdict.

'God knows best, but Joel was never meant for that sweet girl,' Aunt Dora said, 'and I could feel all was wrong when I dreamt of worms the night before the wedding, and when there was a halo round the moon, too.'

Eleven

MA-BOTTLES

Marabastad and winter—inseparable in my mind. Tin and wood shacks leaning in all directions under a pall of smoke from fire-braziers. Lean streets called 'avenues' cutting through, ending up at a fence bordering round a municipal plantation and sewer works from which dull throbs of smell came and lingered over the location. Water dripping from melting dew on roof-tops to describe minute furrows around houses. Fung Prak, the Chinese shopkeeper, coming out on to the veranda with shuffling footsteps under a shrinking body, buckled as if from a chronic but bearable stomach-ache. Abdool coming out, arms folded, chewing eternally as though he'd drop dead if he stopped moving his cat-like jaws. Marabastad in winter.

How vividly I remember some of the whites from whom I fetched washing in the suburbs. Mr. Goldsmith. A middle-aged man with a very red face. He worked at the museum where Aunt Dora's husband also worked. He could easily have carried his bundle of washing to work in his car so that I only went as far as the museum in the centre of the city for it. Perhaps it never occurred to him. Irritable. He cursed aloud if I knocked at his window after a futile attempt to be heard at the door. And then, as I waited under the window, he opened it and hurled the bundle at me and shut the window again. I saw his face after many months of trying to scan it. He seemed consciously to avoid looking at me in the face. He all but threw an envelope containing 12s. 6d. at the end of the month at me. If I reminded him about it he would mutter something, turn around, take the money out of somewhere and stretch out his arm as if he didn't care whether or not it fell in my hands.

Mrs. Reynecke. An Afrikaner with a heavy bosom and dishevelled hair and pudgy hands. She had very little neck and an indifferent supply of buttocks. 'Boy,' she often said at the end of the month, 'tell your mother I'll pay her tomorrow.' That meant any number of days after pay day. We always referred to Mrs. Reynecke as *môre kom*—come tomorrow, which also suggested a system of very heavy farm labour on white people's lands, by which Black men, women and children had to work every day.

Miss Forster was an alcoholic. She looked very old. She was always complaining to me about a number of things that did not concern me. The landlord; the weather; the noise her neighbours made whenever they played 'Boere musiek'—Afrikaner music—on week-ends; her brother in Johannesburg who hadn't sent her money. We called her Ma-Bottles. Every week she sent me to take an order of drinks to a bottle store in town on my way home. I got a shilling for it every time, and so I didn't mind the extra little trouble. Aunt Dora often complained about nasty stains on her underwear. 'As if I don't have enough napkins to wash,' she said.

The one thing for which I always remember the Singer family is their dog and the fuss they made about it. They'd let me wait in the kitchen while Mrs. Singer collected the articles of washing. 'The girl,' as they called their maid, who must have been about twenty-five, gave the dog fresh tea after its breakfast. I often sat there, my mouth flowing with saliva at the warm aroma of coffee and eggs and ham which were foreign down our way. Mrs. Singer was always scolding 'the girl' for not treating the dog well. One day I found another 'girl' working for the Singers. Her predecessor had been sacked for beating the dog. I know that since that time I have never taken well to pets and have always resisted the suggestion of keeping one. At home we christened Mrs. Singer *Chobolo*—shrew.

Bus engines droned and purred and coughed in the chill of a winter morning. Marabastad filed out of their shelters; some trotted with buckled knees as if afraid of breaking something under their feet.

Vapour shot out of the people's mouths, but there was little speaking. They looked like some fate-driven creatures, taking their place in a scheme of things they found; in the same manner in which they cycled down town.

Layers and layers of smoke settled over Marabastad, emphasizing the drabness of those tin houses in the morning light. There was an ironic stability in the temporariness of the workers as they went out the same way as they would come back.

Sharp knees pointed up as old men squatted before fire-braziers with huge depression-stricken birds trussed for roasting; children pushed and jostled one another to draw nearer the fire; little jaws quivered involuntarily to the subtle rhythm of the cold; the men who could stand kept turning round to warm their buttocks and stomachs alternately.

'I'm all right, but this blasted cold. . . .'

'We're not well, all the children have whooping-cough. . . .'

'A drum of boiling water tumbled over two children near the fire, they died as soon as they got to hospital. . . .'

'That's a common winter story. . . .'

'A family of three were found stiff and cold yesterday morning, they had a live brazier in the house all through the night . . . . Dead as my father who lies at Bantule cemetery. . . .'

Winter talk; recurring as sure as the cycle of seasons. Aunt Dora's eldest daughter died that winter. A pot of boiling water that had been sitting screwy on the grid toppled over her as she knelt on the mud floor, warming herself. Died in hospital.

We were playing football with a tennis ball one morning during the school holidays. A number of women were selling cold sweet potatoes, peanuts and home-baked cakes on a patch of grass just near Fung Prak's shop. They came from the country north of Pretoria by ox-wagon, outspanned on open grounds at the end of the location. They cooked their potatoes, and mealies whenever the season came round for either, and came to sell at various points in the location.

One woman had a child on her laps, covered with a dusty-looking frayed blanket. She kept opening the covering as the child coughed violently.

'Boil some *lengana*—wild herb—and give the child to drink,' a woman suggested.

'And let him chew *serokolo*, it will soothe the sores in his chest,' another volunteered.

'My son had the cough,' a woman said from one corner. 'He coughed so your breasts began to itch. I took him to hospital. To look at him you wouldn't think he ever coughed so much.'

'Hospital!' said the woman with the coughing child. 'I went there once and those nurses were rude to me. Slapped me on the bums and shouted at me—Annie, do this, Annie do that—and who cares about children there!'

The woman babbled on as I looked around for a fat sweet potato and whatever else I might like to have.

'You will be all right, my son,' the woman said, adjusting him to a more comfortable position.

I was enjoying the tingling sensation as the sun warmed my blood when we heard stampeding footsteps. In a few seconds policemen had rushed and covered the whole area.

'You people have been warned several times not to sell on the grounds. This is government property and you're making the place dirty.' This was the police commander. There was much of the winter chill in his voice, and something frosty about his face, I thought. The African constable was no less hostile.

'Now, let this be the very last warning,' the commander continued, 'another time all these things will be destroyed and you'll go to prison. Right, pack away and go at once!'

As they left each constable helped himself to an orange here, a steaming sweet potato there and walked off.

I went back to kick the tennis ball. We stopped dead when a wild shriek sounded behind us from among the women who were packing up. '*Jo, Jo-weh!*' Then I saw the woman dash towards our house, which was the nearest. I carried the dish containing her things after her.

I found grandmother and Aunt Dora bending over her. Grandmother took the child from her, and I noticed that he was limp. The mother seemed off her head.

'He's not dead, no, not my son,' she wailed, her hands over her face. 'He must be well and strong again. And when he's big he will go to school. And learn how to write his name and letter to me. But how can I read his letters? I must work very hard and add another ten shillings to that money to buy him a jersey. Then there'll be two. My man is out of work, he's so headstrong he quarrelled with the white man at work, and he should know you don't go far quarrelling with the white man because he is so strong and so rich. My son mustn't die. *Jo, Jo-weh! Me-weh!*'

Aunt Dora was trying to console her.

The child was dead.

Interlude

And there went a man of the house of Levi, and took to wife a daughter of Levi.

And the woman conceived, and bore a son: and when she saw him that he was a goodly child, she hid him three months.

And when she could not longer hide him, she took for him an ark of bulrushes, and daubed it with slime and with pitch, and put the child therein; and she laid it in the flags by the river's brink. And his sister stood afar off, to wit what would be done to him.

And the daughter of Pharaoh came down to wash herself at the river. And her maidens walked along by the river's side; and when she saw the ark among the flags, she sent her maid to fetch it.

And when she had opened it, she saw the child: and, behold, the babe wept. And she had compassion on him and said, This is one of the Hebrews' children.

Then said his sister to Pharaoh's daughter, Shall I go and call to thee a nurse of the Hebrew women that she may nurse the child for thee?

And Pharaoh's daughter said unto her, Take this child away, and nurse it for me, and I will give thee thy wages.

And the child grew, and she brought him unto Pharaoh's daughter, and he became her son. And she called his name Moses: and she said: Because I drew him out of the water.

A 'memory lesson'. Something to be learned off by heart. To know it and to recite it. It's Saturday. No bioscope. Because I must recite it to the teacher on Monday. I know that if I don't know it by Monday, he will lay it on thick with a swish and shout —This must come to an end—his favourite talk. Flat on my tummy on the bank of the river. Just below the police station.

Trying to memorize the passage. Flat on kikuyu grass. There are leafy poplars behind me. The leaves quiver in the lazy midday breeze, causing an interplay of silver and grey and grey. It is good to know and feel close to the earth, its coolness, its kindness; to feel the blue gum trees pour their shade over you.

I'm not afraid here by the stream. Mr. Goldsmith, the white man whose washing we do, is not here. Not even Mrs. Reynecke —*môre kom*, or Mrs. Singer—*Chobolo*. Or even the tottering withered bones of Miss Forster—*Ma-Bottles*. The 'Market Master' with his huge paw is far away, I don't know where. I shan't see Big Eyes and Kuzwi till Monday.

Moses in ark of bulrushes, floating on water. What a beautiful thing to happen to a person to be hidden in a basket. To be so free, so lovable. To be loved and to be fondled and given all you want at the princess's bidding. If I found him among those poplars? I'd run to the police station to report. No, they'd arrest me and lock me up. Just as they did with the man I read of in a scrap of newsprint—the man who was arrested after he had been found with a piece of gold in his pocket, gold he had picked up and thought it should be his. I'd take it to grandmother. No, she would grouse no end. She'd say I've no food to give but it's a nice baby I don't know God in the heavens knows I've no food for one extra mouth so God be my witness take it back where you found it—no, God will provide but have you no work to do without leading me into temptation, boy?

Poor mother! Why wasn't she born a king's daughter? Why didn't she draw me out of the water, out of this water among the poplars. If a baby was fetched from out of a lake, it might as well have been out of this stream. The teacher read the first two verses of the chapter hurriedly and told us to learn from the third verse. A few of us giggled. 'And the woman conceived . . .' he rattled off. Then he frowned. Why don't we learn the first two verses, sir, Rebone asked. This is a Bible not a bioscope story, the teacher said. No use asking what *conceived* means. It's in the Bible, that's what.

No use trying to put the pieces together. Pieces of my life.

They are a jumble. My father's image keeps coming back only to fade. I can't think of him but as a harsh, brutal, cold person. Like his mother. And that brutal limp of his. The smell of the paraffin from the stove and the smell of boiling potatoes and curry. An incident on a Sunday morning. His mother and the mountain. The old woman sitting in the yard, weaving a sleeping-mat or a mat for eating out of. Bending over a stone, grinding corn, her shoulders full of strength, fire and heartlessness. Not the kind of shoulders to sleep on. But the spectre is soon gone. Gone behind the cheerless clouds and torrents of rain and goats scattering in a panic. She's back again to whip an almost bare and moist back because some goats have strayed. A cloudy home-coming.

And then Leshoana river. The cruel river everyone has to cross. Merciless waters beating about the banks, rolling big boulders and trees on its broad back as if in some crude Satanic jest. Dark grey waters frowning at you as you stand on a little rising, not daring to come near, not daring to gaze too long. The deafening roar and long wailing cries along the course: *Mantlalela! mantlalela!*—it's full, it's full. Maybe this little Apies river will be rising as high one day—soon. I seem to hear a mighty roar. I jump into sitting position. No, no fear here. And yet Leshoana is like that. We play blissfully on its white sands, rolling about, feeling their tingling warmth. And then, suddenly we hear the sound of foam bubbles, but not until the water has licked a few of us. Then we jump away in fright, to see a low sheet of water spreading down. And terrified, breathless and foolish laughter among us. How playful violent things can be.

A shrill police whistle. My ribs are aching from lying down. The sun is slanting away. I must go home. Maybe I shall recite those lines about Moses in the bulrushes while I scrape the pots.

Twelve

WITCHCRAFT NEXT DOOR

Aunt Dora was a tough thick-set woman of about twenty-five. She was quick to use a clap on one's cheek. A woman of strict discipline, who wanted things done to time and thoroughly. She had a sharp tongue, and could literally fling a man out who took long before paying a debt for beer. When I had been selling beer in her absence she was quick to find out if I had pocketed a shilling or two when she came back.

We bought malt—ground millet-like corn—and this was mixed with lukewarm water in a drum or four-gallon paraffin tin. A little sour maize meal was put in, and the stuff was left overnight. When it was sour, and fermenting, it was put on a fire to boil. It was put to cool, and then the porridge was put through a strainer. The residue was sold to any horse-keeper like Dinku Dikae the hawker. Straining was the most tricky and anxious stage in the process, and everyone had to be on the look-out for any torch-light or keep his ear to the ground for footsteps. Aunt Dora moved adroitly in and out of the house in spite of her heavy build. Her hips were large, her thick arms worked like pistons. Her thick full lips were a study in concentration. She had beautiful shapely legs which tapered down serenely to the ankles. Her apron became her, lending her bosom a fierce and bold definition. She had a beautiful head, like mother's. Her black hair wasn't half as long as my mother's deep brown hair; her complexion was dark where my mother's was so light that she could have passed for a Coloured woman any time. Aunt Dora carried out all the processes in beer-brewing with lightning speed. Especially when she strained it, there had to be general panic in the house. I had to stand watch outside for the police. Any slip was punishable by flogging or a few stinging claps. She could fling a bar of soap at a person who annoyed her and think nothing of it after. From the First to the Fourteenth Avenue people spoke of her as 'Aunt Dora of Second Avenue'—that woman who throws a man over a fence. If she said: 'Don't come back without that money from Goldsmith' she meant it. Her favourite saying was: 'Love's so concrete it must be bought. I can't love a person who doesn't love me!' My grandmother agreed, apologetically.

She had the inexhaustible pluck to accumulate debts and used her wits to wriggle her way out of the creditors' net. She had a running debt with 'Chipile'—it's cheap—an Indian hawker of soft goods. Every time my aunt bought something Chipile pencilled the amount on the corrugated-iron wall back of the house. How much he depended on this kind of invoicing I could never tell. Often when he came to collect Aunt Dora went to sit in the lavatory. But Chipile would go to the door of the lavatory and say with an indifferent voice: 'Dora, Dora, how long are you going to sit in the lavatory?' In spite of it all the Indian never refused to sell my aunt something new. 'I know you pay, sister,' he said.

Her husband was the direct opposite in temperament. He couldn't be rushed, and the steam my aunt let off never made him blink. I realized this annoyed her all the more and she took it out on us. He was tall and gaunt and his slow manner beat her down.

Two uncles had now gone to boarding institutions, a fact about which grandmother boasted to many. Another uncle still lingered at home, waiting for one of his brothers to complete and send him to an institution.

Grandmother was a religious woman. At fifty she looked younger. I never knew my grandfather, as he died when we were in Pietersburg. But everyone talked endearingly of him. He must have exercised rigid discipline in his house in the true Lutheran fashion, because grandmother liked to quote some of his maxims. He had been a self-taught shoe repairer.

My grandmother ran her house by a no less strict code. We were never allowed to be in the street after dark unless we were on some errand or had got permission to go to evening church service—just a habit we had cultivated. 'That was your grandfather's law,' she said grimly.

Every night we gathered for prayers in the sleeping-room; every morning we were woken up for prayers before we began doing anything. At the end of a prayer, grandmother led us in the Lord's Prayer. Often, by that time, we were asleep on our knees. She loved her friends deeply, hated her enemies passionately. If she didn't like the parents of any of our schoolmates or playmates, she told us so, and discouraged any stable friendship with them. Her frankness was often embarrassing. 'Who are you?' she always wanted to know of any of our mates who visited us. 'Who are your parents?' 'Do you go to church?' She might also say, 'It's the last time I ever want to see you here.'

One morning she had a quarrel with the 'woman next door' as she always called her. '*Sies!*' grandmother hissed and spat at intervals to show her utter contempt. 'What was your mother, after all? She never knew a pin and she used a mimosa thorn to button up her blouse with and she was a heathen and she was not paid a bride price for and you'll remain poor as you are and eat dogs' meat and rats' meat!'

Yet she respected the man next door, because he was a chief's son, although he was not in line of succession. The woman next door was his concubine, and he was grave and I think chief-like. Grandmother always greeted him with respect. *Thulare!* which was the praise name of his tribe. Two allegations against the woman next door that grandmother said 'went against her blood' were that she talked too much and that she 'walked at night', which meant that she practised witchcraft.

After Aunt Dora had had her first baby it fell very ill. On a morning we found a tortoise in the yard. Aunt Dora was beside herself with rage and fear. The woman next door sat outside her house, fat, like a bag of mealie-meal spreading over the back of a donkey. She had a squint, so I could not tell whether she was really looking straight into our passage in the house or not. But perhaps Aunt Dora thought she was. So she paced back and forth in the yard along the fence dividing the two properties, like a caged tigress.

She flung sharp stinging words in a general direction, without daring the woman next door outright. Her enemy continued to sit, facing us, warming her hands over the brazier, somewhat challengingly. Aunt Dora's words narrowed more and more in order to get the woman next door in focus. Still the woman sat, facing us. Her neck was rather too short, and the head and body looked like one stone upon another. In that attitude, she seemed to know at once too much and so little about the tortoise. Which probably annoyed my aunt all the more, for she said: 'And then they sit like brooding hens that seem to know nothing! If my child dies someone will eat her mother. Damn it, these witches make you feel hot between the thighs.'

I could never forget how my aunt looked after that tirade which was like trying to set a wet log of wood on fire. She looked abashed, and wouldn't let her eyes meet ours as we sat on the back stoep. I did not know whether or no to feel sorry for her, because somehow I suspected that the woman next door was responsible for the tortoise being in our yard and for the illness of Aunt Dora's baby. I had the same strong fear of witchcraft as Maupaneng had instilled in me.

Aunt Dora's husband was so much more steady and calm. Aunt Dora spoke in a way that left a sound in one's ear like the spluttering of fat in which a beef steak is frying. He spoke quietly and couldn't be rushed. He was incapable of anything that made a listener writhe or tremble. But then he was incapable of rocking a listener with great wisdom.

Still he exasperated, because he disarmed, anyone who came to him like a steam-roller. My aunt obeyed him implicitly, to the amazement of many. For she often said, 'What's a thing in trousers to me! I could toss it on my little finger and fling it in the dust and roll it around until its price had gone down.' And she meant it. She was regarded by the rest of the family as some sort of chucker-out. And yet she had spent the first eighteen years of her life in the country.

I knew she took unfair advantage of my mother's quiet nature and used her articles of crockery, linen and clothing which she kept in the house since my father left. 'If that limping hyena called Moses had married me instead of you,' she used to say to my mother, 'he'd see trams for flying vultures by the time I'd done with him.'

Partly because my grandmother worshipped cleanliness in the manner she did, and partly because the lavatory looked a horrid mess on week-ends and Monday mornings, we had to take extra trouble to scrub the inside with disinfectant. The bucket was disgustingly full on such days and the floor a pool of urine because there had been many drinking customers at home. We had long given up trying to keep the back and sides of the lavatory clean. Customers invariably came out at intervals, staggered dazedly to the back and sides, leaned against the walls and pissed, their heads resting on their arms in the process. They spat continually, as if they hated the very substance they were letting out. We never succeeded in keeping down the population of maggots that wriggled lustily in the black mud at the back of the lavatory.

Besides our family, the four tenants we had also brewed and sold beer. Grandmother did not allow anyone to brew *skokiaan* because it made the sturdiest of men violently drunk. *Skokiaan* is a drink made by beating compressed yeast in warm water and leaving to ferment. It's deadly, but there are deadlier brews, e.g. pineapple (fermented pineapple mixture); *sebapale-masenke*—one-that-leans-against-the-fence; *bophelo-bontenne*—I-am-tired-of-living. Some of the concoctions contained methylated spirits. The beer brewed at home was made of pure corn malt which was sold freely by the Indians and Chinese. One had to drink many mugs before one got drunk. But then most of the customers bought it expressly to get drunk.

The tenants paid £1 each every month. All house owners in Marabastad paid 14s. rent each month to the municipality, because they had built the shacks themselves, with their own materials.

The oldest male tenant was a roaring drunk. He always joined his wife's customers in a drink. At one time we had a tenant who had a very lazy wife. She got up in the morning and went to sit against the wall in the sun. She let her baby, all greasy and wet, crawl up to her breast, which dangled out of an equally greasy blouse. Flies might buzz around the breast and she wouldn't wave them away. A fly might travel up over her lips to her eyes, but she sat there with stark insensibility. One day I blundered into her room and found her squeezing out milk from her breast into her husband's tea. She was too lazy to stand in the street and wait for a passing milkman, as we all did. 'She needs the flogging of her life,' grandmother remarked. 'She must have sucked from her mother till she was ten,' she added philosophically.

Thirteen

BIG EYES

The Methodist School. Its buildings were no poorer than those put up by other denominations in Marabastad. There were the African Methodist Episcopal School, the Dutch Reformed School, the Anglican School besides. The separatist Lutherans had a rusty old church house but no school. There were a few other separatist churches who leased their buildings to such overflowing schools as the Methodist and the A.M.E. So two kindergarten grades lived outside the main premises of our school.

These consisted of the church hall, built of iron and timber, which housed Standards One, Two and Five. Then there was a detached little brick hall accommodating Standards Three and Four. No class was partitioned off from the others. Then there was another rusty iron-and-timber shanty which always seemed as if it might fall to pieces any moment. This was for Standard Six, the final class of the primary school. All these buildings had wooden floors with loose boards that screamed and groaned painfully under human feet.

We sat three on a small desk in each class. Blackboards rested on easels and had peeled off badly. But the teachers retained a certain respectability as they wrote boldly on the boards, trying to be legible. And there was a continuous shower of chalk dust coming down in the process.

Monday morning. The day when Big Eyes, the principal, always came to assembly in the church hall with renewed ferociousness which one couldn't miss in those ever-dilated eyes. Because Monday was a day of reckoning for Big Eyes: the day when week-end sinners were caned, in the presence of the school assembly. There were those he had caught at a Saturday dance, or Sunday afternoon party; those he had caught love-making or standing at a street corner in an attitude he suspected, in the glare of his big torchlight, to be one of love-making; those who had been absent from the Friday afternoon scouts' parade. Often Big Eyes dressed up like a woman and dropped in at a dance or night party. That way he netted his fish. They paid dearly for it on Monday. And he knew his teenage pupils thoroughly, although we were over 300 in classes one to six.

'That's a schoolmaster for me,' said a number of residents. . . .

'Give me the man who'll clean the streets of human scum,' said others.

'That's right! We see today growing before us a new kind of boy and girl,' some said. 'Cheeky, no respect for their parents, go to the Columbia, bear children before their eyes are open. There's the headmaster to help us!'

Grandmother applauded Big Eyes's performance. But the applause came to an abrupt stop when he caned me for having been absent from a joint school choir practice. The choir, like the police and other civil servants, was exercising for the visit of the late Prince George, Duke of Kent, to South Africa. That was in 1934. I had then just graduated into Standard Six. I could not attend the practice because I had gone to fetch washing from the suburbs. Big Eyes didn't accept the excuse. Grandmother wanted to explain my punishment away. But Aunt Dora, who was always quick to take offence if she thought the way she ordered her life was being undermined, took up cudgels. When she dragged me alongside her to school on Tuesday morning a number of Indian and Chinese shopkeepers, who lined Barber Street, showed amusement and curiosity. Abdool quickly spat out whatever he was chewing, his stomach overshooting the edge of his veranda, and called to his associate in the shop. Elisha, his father, mumbled something through his beard. 'What's wrong, *mosadi*—woman?' Sung Li, the Chinaman, said, pulling in his mucus in order to spit it out. Aunt Dora just kept her course, towing me behind her all the time.

'Why did you beat Es'ki yesterday, Principal, when he told you he'd taken washing away?' she asked Big Eyes.

'What shall I do if every pupil gives a reason for not coming to practice?'

'I thought I was talking about Es'ki, I don't care what you do with the other children.'

'God's woman, this is a difficult time and we must get these songs known before the Prince comes.'

'Oh, so washing must not be fetched because the Prince is coming: will he give me food?'

'Can't the boy fetch it another day?' Secretly, I'd rather be at choir practice than in suburban streets delivering or fetching washing. And I wanted so much to be in a choir that was going to be listened to by masses of people in front of a big man from Britain. And as I stood there beside my aunt, I was hoping desperately that she would appoint another day for the suburbs. Thursday or early Saturday.

'No, he can't,' said my aunt tersely. 'You had no right to punish the boy before you found out if he was telling the truth.'

Big Eyes jerked his head backward in astonishment. 'I know how to run my school, madam.' His nostrils opened and narrowed like bellows.

'Let me run my house the way I want, and I don't do it by using a cane on innocent children. The boy's as good as mine. My sister left him in my care.'

'The church left the school in my care, madam.'

'Another time it happens I'll have to speak to the Superintendent. Now go to your class, Es'ki.' I left. I could hear Big Eyes say, 'We'll see.'

The superintendent of every church school was usually the white minister who served the European congregation in town and through whom the Government sent its instructions to the African schools under his denomination.

I was to keep to my schedule for delivering washing. But when the Prince came, to be in the scout division that did the march past at the race-course was exciting enough; we also enjoyed the cold drinks and buns that were doled out to us. It was a 'Non-Europeans Only' affair, as there had been a 'Europeans Only' day.

I had passed Standard Five at the age of 15 under a tall teacher who had a very clumsy gait, long arms he didn't seem to know what to do with, and rusty rotted teeth. For the first time in my primary school career I felt self-confident. In Standard Five Rebone and I competed for first place, and we alternated, as if by mutual consent, in first and second places.

I still hated arithmetic. My passion for reading grew stronger. The white family for whom my mother worked gave me old newspapers and periodicals. They merely shrugged their shoulders when my mother told them why I wanted the papers. More than that, they showed no interest. I was disappointed. I thought naïvely that if they were superior to me and my kind they should show some interest in a less fortunate creature who wanted to acquire something like the degree of literacy they enjoyed. Even if it were the kind of interest that might prompt one to retort: 'Say, he reads English!' Yes, I was very proud to be able to read English.

My mother was proud, very proud of me in my progress. She could never afford to buy me any books outside the two reading books necessary in the school, one in the vernacular and the other in English. I continued to rummage for discarded, coverless, rat-eaten, moth-eaten, sun-creased books for my reading. It was during the blind quest that I stumbled on a tattered copy of *Don Quixote*—an old translation. I must have read it three times over. The leaves fell out in the process.

When Big Eyes left Pretoria there were all sorts of ugly stories about why he left. But Marabastad parents generally clung to his departing shadow and cried, 'Who will look after our children?' None of us boys and girls knew why he left. There were no farewells either. He just slipped out of our lives. All we knew was that he had gone to work in Johannesburg and not as a teacher any more. But after he left, there was a void. Monday mornings at assembly was like all other days. Times when we made noise in class we shot glances towards the window, half-expecting to see those big eyes roving over us, seeming to pop out of the head that rested its chin on the window-sill.

A tall slender man from eastern Transvaal came to head the Methodist School. He was a much softer man. He did not have the stentorian voice and forbidding face of Big Eyes. Kuzwi stuck to his post in Standard Four. One teacher had died of tuberculosis, others had left and been replaced.

In Standard Six I felt as if a great light of dawn had flashed into me. In spite of harassing conditions at home, my school career was taking on a definite shape. What had earlier on been a broad and obtuse shaft of light, was narrowing, sharpening and finding a point of focus. As far as my performance in various subjects was concerned, I was well ahead of my classmates—in every subject but arithmetic. Later Rebone dropped three places lower. 'Told you she couldn't last', said the bigger boys. I knew why: her father's hawking business was ailing. Vegetable and fruit prices were rising at the market, and Dinku Dikae felt throttled. I also knew that every night Rebone taught her father how to read, write and calculate simple arithmetic. Because of this, she could sense some of the most delicate variations of mood in her father. She told me all about it.

'You know,' she said one day, 'Father is simply scared of the police. Can't do his lessons for the evening if a policeman so much as crossed the road before his trolley passed. Afraid the policeman's going to stop him.'

'I'm terribly afraid of a policeman, too,' I said. 'In Pietersburg I'd hide behind a bush to look at a policemen pass on horseback. All the time I simply felt he knew I was hiding. That shining badge, those big muscles and bone in the horse. They made my throat ache with fear. And then the Saturday night—you remember when—' She nodded impatiently.

'You're never afraid of anything, you,' I said.

'Me? I'm afraid of dying.' We laughed.

There had grown up a close friendship between Rebone and Flu'. They both didn't have mothers, Rebone's having died just before they moved to Pretoria.

Two favourite poems I still remember vividly preparing for the inspector who came for oral examinations were Tennyson's *Half a league, half a league* and Byron's *The Destruction of Sennacherib's Host*. We just revelled in the heroism expressed in the lines. European inspectors insisted that we use action while we recited, and pupils sent themselves into all sorts of facial and muscular contortions to impress the educational officers. So impressed were we, including the teacher, with our own performance, that we carried poetry to the concert stage. We shouted and barked at the audience. We leapt forward to show how 'the Assyrian came down like a wolf on the fold', and stamped on the floor, and I think we drowned our voices. I now wonder how many understood what we were about. We understood little of what we were reciting ourselves. Often we asked the teacher to explain some of the lines; he simply said, 'It's poetry, boys and girls, it's poetry, can't you see?' We left it at that, feeling awed.

Fourteen

THE COLUMBIA DANCE HALL

For all that it mattered, the depression of the early thirties did not seem on the surface to add an ounce of pressure more to the poverty of the Black man.

We still had one tarred street for the police to patrol and for the white superintendent of the location to drive his sleek shining car along. There were still a few electric lights dotted about street corners and none in the houses; the smell from the sewerage centre in the plantation below us still came in a suffocating wave. Of course fewer of us went to the Dougall Hall bioscope because the market and the golf links were scantier and the white people didn't want to pay as much as they used to. They brought the price down from nine pence to six pence for carrying vegetables five miles to Sunnyside suburb. Children still squatted in the street to relieve themselves, chickens still came to peck at the stools with relish.

There was much less to eat at home, and boys and girls of our age group raided Indian hawkers' backyards for discarded fruits, bread and vegetables in garbage bins. But then we had always done that after school. We planned our strategy of entering through the back gate. Some of the hawkers were vicious with the sjambok, especially Cassim Hassim. Some of the women connived at our acts; others poured rice crust and water on us from the balconies, just to have a laugh. Often we looked up to the balconies and laughed with them while we shook down rice grains from out of our shirts. We returned to rummage again. Little Links and Danie, the noisiest boy down Second Avenue whom we could seldom trust to 'pull off a job' with a sense of duty becoming a Fox, raided one yard. Ratau and China went to

Moosa's wholesale establishment for 'tin-my-Moosa'. This meant that they would ask Moosa to off-load vats of bananas from a truck and get a tin of black-skinned overripe bananas for it. Ratau was the quietest and steadiest of us and said little; China came of parents who always dressed smartly and were reputed to be well off. For Ratau this was a 'decent' assignment, and for China—a kind of sport. Moloi and Isaac, the round-faced boy who came from Bantule, another location two miles away, and I, struck elsewhere. Isaac attended school with us and preferred to play with the Foxes. And so we fanned out over the Asiatic Bazaar.

At the end of the raid we met at the river, just below the police station, with a good haul of oranges, sponspecks, carrots, tomatoes, bananas and other items: all rotten in parts. We went to the tap at the corner of the police tennis court and washed off as much rot as we could. After the meal we got dry sticks and ran them the whole length of the corrugated-iron wall of Fung Prak the Chinaman's yard. He made malt and sold it to the local shops for illicit home beer-brewing in the locations. Our little game annoyed his vicious bulldog inside and it followed the rat-tat-tat, barking ineffectually all the time. There were days when we divided the booty and took it home.

Twice a week we took sacks and made a long journey to the municipal ash dump in the last suburb west of town. There we scratched and scrounged for coke for use in our home braziers. We came back all white with ash. And when we washed our cracked scaly feet, we felt like dancing a jig from the stinging pain when the feet dried.

It was during those years that I began to regard the Indian as someone who was also privileged to have more money than us or the Coloured people. He traded among us, and yet he kept aloof from our sufferings, unmoved by them. He appeared to me, in those years, as somebody who could never suffer; who didn't die; who couldn't cry or care. We laughed and joked with him in his shop; he played with the breasts of some of our girls just to annoy them; we called each other pet names; but it seemed that we could never project ourselves into each other's lives and share certain things. But then we didn't care to. The Chinaman, on the other hand, was a surly, disgruntled creature who just dragged his feet about and moved with a sinister stoop. How could we not believe our parents when they told us never to venture beyond the counter of a Chinaman's shop because he ate human flesh? Fung Prak's tiny wife would stand on her veranda until customers came in. She stood there, her arms folded, laughing at the heavy-booted African policemen marching past, their buttocks stretching the slit at the back of the coat. She hardly had any buttocks. There she was, her lower teeth receding as her upper row was advancing; and as she turned to walk into the shop the hem of her dress clung to the woollen stockings, on one leg and then on the other.

I couldn't consciously probe into the attitudes of the Asiatics; I simply felt a barrier beyond a certain point of contact.

There were other and deeper changes at work in Marabastad, in Bantule to the west of us, in Lady Selborne, six miles farther, in Cape Location next to the Asiatic Bazaar, and in the peri-urban locations east of town. Boys of our age were getting rough and knife-happy. Scores of them left school and joined the won't-works and some of those who had lost their jobs. They stood about on shop verandas, made rude jokes and guffawed with broken voices, chewed bubble-gum impudently and smoked insolently. Boeta Lem (Brother Blade) from down our street easily collected a nice bunch of hangers-on about him. They hero-worshipped him as an ex-convict. They brought him food and money from their homes. They spoke a lot about the wonderful performance of their counterparts 'on the Rand'. Somewhere in the Golden City, we felt, big evil things were going on. And our parents blamed it all on this mystical bond.

'If I see you again listening to what that Boeta Lem says, I'll chop your neck into pieces, pieces, pieces with an axe!' grandmother warned us. 'He's a heathen, his mouth smells like the sewerage down in those trees. His father can't do a thing with him any more, and heathen too, if you want to know. All he does is sit there in his house, kill lice between his nails just because his son would rather go about sweeping God's streets with his tattered trousers and go about rooting in garbage cans instead of working. He doesn't even know which way the church door's facing by Titus who lies in his grave. Both of them will soon be eating rats and dogs.' Titus was my grandpa, her late husband.

Marabastad seemed to be turning inside out, showing all her dirty underwear. 'The world is coming to an end,' grandmother said with a sigh. 'as sure as Titus sleeps in his grave. What we see today is a sign of God's anger. When I was young there wasn't so much hate; boys and girls didn't insult their elders like this; and we helped one another during famine. The world is nearing an end.' She frightened me that way.

'Nonsense, Hibila,' Old Rametse from the lower end of the street said, 'this is the beginning of a new world. I worked for a white farmer, Van Wyk his name was. "Petros," he used to say, "listen here, Outa,[1] if ever your children go to the city, know it's the end of them. My son Koos is long gone, and now Grieta's going, and I know they're lost. But thank God in the heavens they come of an upright and God-fearing house. If they throw away their Bible teaching, God forgive them. I've written to Dominee Brink at the Groote Kerk to look after them." ' Old Rametse chuckled. 'Ah, Hibila, that Van Wyk was a kind man but still a big Baas. I've been here now—let me see—ten plus five years—how many?—fifteen, and only last year I saw young Koos in town with a girl hanging on his arm. They were both drunk but not so bad. He's a fellow with a big shadow now, and you think he'd know me? Ha-ha, I stopped him and I said, Greetings, Kleinbaas, remember Petros from the farm? I saw in those eyes that he remembered me, but he said, "Get out of my way, Kaffir!" and he passed on. Now I ask you, Hibila, if the white man goes on like this and he has everything, farms money, good clothes, clean face, what were you and I—we who live on borrowed things? Give me that mug of coffee, my boy.' It was a special privilege he enjoyed, to be given coffee in our home. When I

[1] Used by the Afrikaans for Black male servants like Aia for maids. Also used for any African with a tone of contempt.

wasn't feeling so good, as often happened when he was around, he reminded me.

'Borrowed things, borrowed things,' Aunt Dora said after he had left. 'He thinks we were born yesterday. Everybody knows he has a lot of money hidden somewhere. And yet such a miser too. Look at the khaki clothes he wears—a man with so much money.'

No one really knew how rich old Rametse was, if that was true. But people spoke of it as a fact. A few days later he came to our house waving his arms madly. 'You've never seen such a thing. That *skelm*[1] has done it again. It's me this time. Son of a rat, son of a pig, son of a heathen, son of a baboon, son of a crocodile without a name, son of a runaway mother!'

'Who's that?' grandmother asked.

'That piece of filth called Boeta Lem. Stole all my money from under my mattress. My woman saw him, saw him run out of the house, saw him with her eyes. I've worked for years for my money, long before his mother carried that lump of sin in the womb. His hands are getting mouldy in his pockets because instead of doing honest work he wants to ruin other people. Little Shepherd, he has taken my life away with the money!'

'Go to the police station,' Aunt Dora suggested.

'Where do you think I'm going?'

Aunt Dora laughed secretly. He made his way out towards the police station, talking aloud and gesticulating. 'Modisana!'[2] he kept saying.

The police did not or could not prosecute, although the Blade was taken to the station. 'God's no fool. He'll stumble and fall one day. You'll see.' That was grandmother's ruling. Ma-Lebona, Ma-Janeware, and even the cross-eyed woman next door, said grandmother couldn't have been more right. 'God will deal with him.' Old Rametse's story of how much had been stolen changed much. He said it was five pounds, then twenty, then ten. And still people didn't know how rich or poor he was.

[1] Afrikaans for *rascal* now worked into Sotho languages.
[2] Little Shepherd—Jesus.

It seems God did catch up with the Blade. One Saturday night he raped a teen-aged girl in a dark field near the Dougall Hall. He had forced the girl, at the point of a knife, from the door of the cinema to the field. The girl ran home to report, and the police got on Boeta Lem's tracks. He was picked up at the Columbia. He still had the girl's knickers in his pocket.

The next week, on a Sunday, Second Avenue residents swarmed at the gate of the Blade's home, where he lived with his father and stepmother. The people were angry. He had been bailed out, and they didn't like it. Aunt Dora went, not grandmother, who said she was sorry her leg was sore, otherwise she'd go and tell 'the heathen Blade a thing or two, roll him in the dust a few times and lower his price on the market.'

'Let him come out!'

'Let us see him!'

'We don't want animals here!'

'What, he gets a lawyer to speak for a criminal!'

'And it's his father, he knows his son's a criminal!'

'He's giving his son more pluck to do bigger crimes!'

'That lad will kill another man yet God's my witness!'

'What is it you want to do with the lad?' Old Rametse asked a knot of people at one end.

'Are *you* going to ask that, you whose money he stole?'

'I know, but I also want to know why I should be here.'

'We want to take him back to the police station. They must keep the dog chained until it goes to court.'

Old Rametse nodded understandingly.

'Speak to his father,' said the Blade's stepmother, panting and waving her apron this way and that as if to disown the Blade.

At last the father came out of his hovel, his son's hand in the grip of his, sinewy and trembling.

'Speak to them, speak to them,' the stepmother babbled, her fat hands fidgeting with the hem of the apron. 'I've long been talking about this boy of yours. I'm weary of it, Jehovah knows in the heavens. Speak to them.'

'God's people!' the man began. The noise gradually subsided.

I always remember how dignified the Blade's father looked on that day, even in the state of agitation.

'God's people!' he repeated, 'what do you want of me?'

'We want your son, he must go back to the police cells,' a woman said.

'That's right,' another echoed. 'You've no right to keep a criminal in your house!'

'And even hire a lawyer for him.'

'If he'd raped a white girl he'd have been kept locked up until he should hang.'

'You must deliver him.'

For a few minutes Boeta Lem's father seemed lost for words. Then, 'God's people, hear me. You men and women here have children. You're lucky some of them are not like this lad here. You're lucky some of them haven't raped and stolen. It hurts me when a boy of my own blood makes life miserable for other people. For every stab he gives a victim I get a hundred in my heart, not so easy to heal. You say if I'm willing to pay a lawyer to try to set him free, it means I like the dirty crime he has committed, and others before that.'

He paused, and I could see he was weeping. His son stood there beside him, with a dirty sleeved vest for a shirt, and a wide flannel bag for trousers, out of which his long bare toes peeped. He looked both frightened and defiant.

'Whoever thinks that is a cruel person. Why do I hire a lawyer then? I don't know. I can't tell you.'

'What about my money?' Old Rametse said, his Adam's apple pushing out sharply, and the sinews and veins in his neck telling a story of pain.

'That is a matter for the police, Son of Rametse,' the Blade's father said. 'I've brought him outside with me so that he should know what people think of his wickedness.'

A wave of mumbling swept through the crowd, and they dispersed, threatening doom, predicting chaos, invoking God's instruments of punishment. 'We leave you to chain your own dog then,' one said, throwing up his arms.

Boeta Lem subsequently appeared in court. He was sentenced to ten years' hard labour.

'You see,' grandmother said. 'They hanged a man for doing what a white woman asked him to do in her own bed, and this is what they do to us! You go away from here, Es'ki, or you'll be telling your mates fat lies after hearing this!' I took myself off.

Columbia Hall cuddled in the centre of a row of Indian houses in the Asiatic Bazaar, just wedged between Marabastad and the Cape Coloured Reserve. It was an old building, with sooty walls that were painted and repainted time after time to give the deception of attractiveness. On either side of the low platform that was meant to be a stage, was a door leading to a lounge room that covered the breadth of the hall in length and was partitioned into cubicles, each fitted with a couch. The lights of the Columbia were never bright.

We often did odd jobs in the hall for the manager for pocket money, and breathlessly we examined every part of the interior. Breathlessly, because few parents liked the sound of the name 'Columbia'. We were told in doubtful terms that it was an evil place where immoral practices went on behind the cloak of a dance or concert. Boys who were not tethered to their homes told us gleefully what dancers and concert performers did in the cubicles backstage. The men paid money for the convenience of using the couches with their girls. At the sight of the couches, my head turned round, aflame with all sorts of pictures, and I promised myself the opportunity of finding out what it was grandmother and Aunt Dora didn't want us to see. That is, if I should get the chance of attending a function.

The opportunity came. Talking pictures had just arrived in Pretoria. A new Indian-owned bioscope hall, the Star Picture Palace, opened for the first time in the Asiatic Bazaar with a showing of *The Singing Fool*, featuring Al Jolson. Excited crowds flocked at the cinema to see the new wonder in the history of the film.

We were permitted to go—my little uncle and I, escorted by an older uncle and Aunt Dora. Every night there was something on at the Columbia. What better night could there be for going there? But then I doted on the movies, and it would break my heart to hear the other boys recall among themselves what they had seen at the Picture Palace. I had a little money I had made at the market, and I could afford the admission fee of a shilling at the Columbia. So, once I had been given my ticket, I lost myself in the crowd and dashed to the Columbia just round the block. There would be an introductory programme of shots and a silent film before Al Jolson.

I was let into the Columbia. I came face to face with the U-NO-MES dance band, whose music had before only floated to our ears as we passed the hall; violently, noisily, but vigorously. Thinking back on it now I remember the sad note of depravity, self-abandon, sweet, sensuous dissipation 'Marabi' jazz sounded. The small jazz combos like U-NO-MES and the Merrymakers beat out a new two-to-the-bar jazz, the second note in which was accentuated by a bang on the drum. The name 'Marabi' came from *Marabastad*. From there it went to the Reef. Handbills in pink or green or white could be seen on electric poles and rusted corrugated-iron walls which read:

THINGS ARE UPSIDE-DOWN!
AND WHY? 'CAUSE THERE'S GALORE SENSATIONAL,
FANTASTICAL, SCINTILLATING, REVERBERATING
JAZZ EXTRAVAGANZA
BRING YOUR GAL, SPIN YOUR GAL FOR THE
PALPITATING MARABI RHYTHM OF U-NO-MES
AT A
DAYBREAK DANCE AT COLUMBIA EVERY NIGHT

I stood against the wall in that misty hall of dim lights. Couples clung to each other very tightly, swayed sideways and backwards and forwards at the hips. Their faces were wet with perspiration. Occasionally a man or girl wiped it off with the back of the hand. They swayed to the monotonous tune, seeming to hear or see nothing, lost in the savagery of the band's music. They might even be blissfully unaware of the fact that just round the block, Al Jolson was bringing the magic of the age—the sound film. I continued to stand there, drinking in all the dust that rose from the concrete floor, the dim lights, the smell of perspiration and tobacco smoke. That was the Columbia, the name that spelled horror and damnation to those who concerned themselves with human conduct. Then I saw them. The couples, dancing through the doors to the lounge backstage, clinging to each other, carrying and pushing each other along.

I felt a solid lump shoot up and then down my throat. The palms of my hands were damp with sweat against the wall. And I dashed out and made for the cinema, my knees shaking from a feeling of guilt. If any of my people should find out. . . .

I enjoyed Al Jolson all the same. A few weeks later we saw Charlie Chaplin's *City Lights*. TALKING, SINGING, DANCING became familiar labels on cinema hoardings. At first, I was a little uneasy at the prospect of going out of business. The boys wouldn't need my services any more as reader of the titles on the screen. They'd have to listen to the dialogue. But soon I drowned my little fears in the novelty and expediency of it all.

That was the Marabastad of the depression years. In spite of poverty, the people found other outlets for the urge for recreation, besides the Columbia. More jazz troupes sprang up. On public holidays a horse-drawn cart might come down Barber Street with an old piano on it and about four other instrumentalists, playing Marabi just for the love of it and a troupe would be singing *Happy Days are Here Again*, *Tip-toe to the Window*. It was grand to dream of unknown tulips, roses, lazy lagoons, mandolins in Santa Lucia, beautiful ladies in blue, old Father Thames, the unknown sunny side of the street. The same thing happened on New Year's Day. Picnic groups were formed, and the fun started only when they were arriving back home. Each company had its own band and uniform. There were the Sunbeams, Sonny-Boys (which included girls), Callies, Red-White-And-Dizzy (*dizzy* meant *green*). These names corresponded with the football teams the parties were attached to. When they arrived in lorries and toured the location and displayed their colours, their plumage wasn't that of depression-stricken birds at all.

Preachers in church spoke vehemently against immorality. They denounced places like the Columbia and foretold eternal punishment. And they collected the endless dues from the people: money for the monthly ticket; money for the quarterly ticket; money for the half-yearly ticket; money for Holy Communion; money for the minister's journey to a conference; money to build a church in some outlandish area or another; money for the minister's bicycle. 'We're poor, we have no money any more,' people said. But they brought something and laid it on the table. And regularly the white superintendents came to preach sermons. Every church except the A.M.E. had a white minister as overseer. And when they did come, the congregations turned up in full force to listen to the white preacher. The stewards and the church councillors were more correct and officious than usual on such days, keeping up a tight-jawed look of responsibility. Stout prayer women looked immaculate with their dazzling red blouses and white starched hats. But the dazzle of these colours was toned down by the sleek, shining black shawls they had on. How very much of birds the women reminded me!

There was a surge of revival services in the various churches. Grandmother herded us and left my brother, sister and me in the Methodist church hall, as our mother was Methodist because my father was nominally one. Then grandmother, Aunt Dora and the rest of the family went to the Lutheran Church, because my grandfather had been Lutheran. The night of the eve of Good Friday, Lutheran women sang from street to street, waking up their church members, singing all the time. The music jolted us out of our sleep and we rubbed our eyes and sat up until the last chords of that grave music could be heard faintly in the distance, and we slumped back into sleep.

But church attendance generally dropped those days. And the preachers blamed loose morals for it. The depression was God's punishment, they said. Women, old men and children of our age kept up their attendance. The young men and women stayed away. The old men slept most of the time. Most of the time we looked at the women, at the preacher and then at the sleeping old men.

There was more beer drinking. More boys and girls left school and had children. And the preacher pointed a large finger at us who remained, mute, helpless, tethered to some family custom and honour. In spite of Boeta Lem's absence, 'bright boys', as they called themselves, didn't go slow. Instead, they broke up into rival gangs: XY Ranch; Jumbo Ranch; Frisco Ranch; Texas Ranch; Express Ranch; Uppercut Ranch. They stopped men in the street and undressed them completely at the point of a knife and left them naked. The clothes were sold. The boys raped and robbed.

At this time, I acquired the passion to roam from one church to another on different Sundays. I just loved change; it was so refreshing, and I could listen to a sermon painlessly coming from different preachers. I loved the music of the Lutherans. It didn't have the monotonous pattern of many of the Methodist and A.M.E. hymns. I loved the incense and regalia in the Anglican church; I found fun in listening to the A.M.E. pastor who liked to mix English and Sotho in a sermon. 'That man is mad,' grandmother said. 'The day his gods descend upon him and ask him where he has thrown his mother tongue, he'll scream.' I just thought he was funny. And then I was constantly amused by the way in which he wound bits of string round his ears to hold his eye-glasses because they were old and broken.

There was a tiny iron enclosure housing a small congregation calling themselves the Gaza Church. I couldn't summon enough courage to go to it. During those years of the depression a number of people went about claiming to be prophets and faith healers. Nzama, the pastor of Gaza, was such a 'prophet'. On Good Friday each year he entered a deep hole in the plantation below his church, at the lowest end of our location. He stayed there and 'rose' on the third day—Easter. Some said he went through the period without food; some that his wife sent him blankets and food when no one was looking. But Nzama and his congregation claimed that he actually died and rose because he had the powers of Christ.

Another time a woman took her paralysed son to Nzama for

faith healing. Nzama went through his ritual, and when the patient didn't respond, he set about cutting the stiff and contracting sinews of the ankles and the knees. The child died and Nzama was arrested and jailed. I shuddered at the thought of venturing into Gaza. I didn't.

I told grandmother about my wanderings. She said I'd end up by attending no church at all. 'Heathen like your useless father.' The accent she always put on the word 'heathen' didn't have the same ugly forebodings it used to. 'I suppose you'll soon be wanting to go to that tent church up the avenue. I'd cut off your head for you, I'd cut you into pieces, pieces, pieces.'

The tent church up the street was an institution of the depression years. Pastor M'Kondo came with his sickly wife from Alexandra Township in Johannesburg. They had broken away from the Methodist Church of South Africa. His was said to be a branch of what was commonly known as the Donkey Church. Its emblem was a picture of Christ entering Jerusalem on a donkey. Bishop Ramushu of the new church was noised about as a most powerful preacher. His mother church had raised one of the several categories of dues from 2s. to 2s. 6d. He had protested to the white authorities, but they were adamant. He left and took with him thousands of members.

Soon the local Anglican priest, Pitso, pulled out of his church with a large following. This was after a quarrel with the Bishop of Pretoria. He formed his church called the African Catholic Church. But he later felt so bad about it that he took the people back to the Anglican Church. He was sent away to some distant place to do penance, and was never again seen in Pretoria.

Hundreds of young men and women were drifting into Pretoria from the northern Transvaal. Occasionally I met some of the men who were big boys when we were at school together in Pietersburg. These men worked as domestic servants in the suburbs.

On Sundays they came down from the suburbs as far away as seven miles from Marabastad, to Bantule on the other side. They had their playgrounds there. A bare grassy patch where they boxed bare-fisted. On such days we went out of our houses to look at them in rival batches, march up Barber Street. They had on shorts, tennis caps, tennis shoes, and handkerchiefs dangled from their pockets. They crouched, shook their fists in the air so that their plastic bangles round the wrists clanged. They moved with long strides like a black army, and their legs glistened with petroleum jelly or soap grease which they smeared carefully after washing. It was a common saying that when they sprang and shouted and crouched like that, their 'blood was boiling'—literally—and they were in vicious mood. Every Sunday white mounted police escorted them to Bantule.

At the playground they formed a ring and rivals went in in couples for a gruelling, bloody and savage bout. Anyone could go in and challenge someone from an opposition stable. That was the kind of boxing we liked to do on the white sands of Leshoana river in the tropical moonlight, when I lived in the north.

These people came to be known as *malaita*—Sotho for *ruffians*. When they dispersed, the police got close on their heels and beat them on their backs with sjamboks. This seemed to make the *malaita* mad. For they scattered and took different roads to town. Some went through Marabastad, some through the Indian and Coloured Reserves. The police were supposed to prevent their entering these locations, but they were so brutal in the use of the sjamboks that it had the opposite effect.

The *malaita* assaulted people who crossed their path, raped women and girls. Once they castrated a man at the river below us. The residents feared and hated them, and none of us ever expressed pity for them as the constables lashed at them with sjamboks, or drove their horses over them, laughing all the time. We delighted in chasing after them with sticks and stones. We followed them until they reached the centre of town. And still the *malaita* left their masters' houses every Sunday afternoon to go through the same experience every time!

Fifteen

FIGHT WITH ABDOOL

Pretoria has always been a tough Jim Crow town. No better than the outside *dorps* in any of the provinces. Some of the English families my mother worked for from time to time were patronizing towards me. Others resisted me. She worked for a Dr. Broderick once. His children often came to me or called, 'John, you want Eva?' Eva was my mother, John was not my name. Or 'Eva, here's your son.' Then they looked me up and down, faces screwed up, eyes squinted. Sometimes they tossed me an orange. I never got used to being examined like that. I resented it but at the same time feared that any moment the children might decide to tell their parents that I was undesirable. Apparently they didn't. But after a time I just went straight to lean against the side wall of my mother's little room and waited until she should come out of the big house. She continued to work for English families. She always refused to learn Afrikaans and she spoke English with ease although with a number of errors; most of it self-taught through working continuously for English-speaking families. We spoke northern Sotho at home and a mixture of Afrikaans and Sotho outside.

The Afrikaans people for whom Aunt Dora washed made no bones about the fact that they didn't want me to get into their kitchen. Their children merely peeped through a window. Otherwise, I didn't seem to exist. I felt easier that way. If a child wanted to let the mother know I was about, it said, 'Ma, die wasgoed-kaffir is hier—Mummy, the washing Kaffir has come.' And the child took no more notice of me.

I came to learn the hard way that one had to keep out of the white man's way. There was enough hardship in my home without deliberately waiting to absorb the cruder impacts from our surroundings. So if a group of whites walked, as they invariably did, abreast of one another on pavements, we gave way. In a sense we were happy enough that we could visit public places like the Museum, the Zoo, the Union Buildings and so on, on certain days only, when the whites would not be there as well. We Blacks were not even tolerated near the fence of a park. Such places were foreign to us, and so we loved to stand with our faces pressed against the wire fence, to admire and envy white children playing on swings and 'horses'. To us they were performing a feat, and we often shouted to congratulate them on their antics. When we were barked away by the white caretaker, I hated him, and hated the children and envied them.

But whites who liked to could enter public places on days set aside for Blacks: usually week-days and Sunday mornings, up to 12 noon. A couple were sitting near each other under a tree on a day the Foxes had decided to raid the Zoo. The couple spoke Afrikaans. Danie, Ratau and I stopped to watch a monkey on a tricycle. 'Ag, don't, Blikkies!' the white girl said, laughing hysterically. We cast furtive glances to see what was happening. It was evident that the man Blikkies was not very sober. He sat with his legs folded under him. The girl was on her knees, putting her hair in order. Her face was flushed up to the ears. Blikkies took her into his arms, laid her on her stomach on his lap, spanked her a few times, gently, and let her go. She laughed, and kept saying, 'Don't, don't, Blikkies. *Ag, Sies!*' He drove his finger in between her buttocks, pushing in her dress as he did so. This seemed to propel her in a forward movement, and he followed behind, both of them on their knees. The man Blikkies kept his finger in the same area, while the girl, obviously tickled, laughed in shrill tones, crying, '*Eina*, Blikkies, *Eina*, Blikkies, *Eina! Ag* don't, man *ag sies!*' And she laughed at intervals.

The three of us nudged one another and giggled. The couple got up and moved towards us, the man Blikkies staggering slightly.

'Kick me a Kaffir tonight, Blikkies,' the girl said, looking murderously civil. I remembered that during their little act our eyes met for a few seconds, hers and mine. 'Kick me a Kaffir tonight, *my lief*, won't you, my love? A nice kick on the arse of a nice black Kaffir monkey, eh?'

'Tonight, my little heart? Why not now?'

He came towards us. 'What are we looking for?' he said. He swung his leg and missed Danie who was always agile. The man Blikkies' hoof struck the monkey's iron railings, and he fell, buckling from obvious pain. We bolted away. From behind the elephant we realized the monkey had stopped his tricycle antics, as if in deference to Blikkies, whom the girl was trying to help up.

Within a few moments all the Africans cleared that part of the gardens. 'Beware of the white man, he's very, very strong,' my mother often said. And all the years of my boyhood the words rang in my head.

December 16th was Dingaan's Day. A public holiday meant to commemorate the death of Piet Retief and his men at the hands of 'treacherous Dingaan', the Zulu king and Shaka's brother.

It was common for Afrikaners on Dingaan's Day to parade along Church Street in the centre of Pretoria on horseback. They wore Voortrekker clothing and large-brimmed hats and big broad bandoliers. It was quite a spectacle as these men, some of them Anglo-Boer War veterans, grimly filed down the street, obviously admired by the large crowds of whites on the sidewalks and rooftops.

I came from the suburbs that Dingaan's Day of 1934, when I saw these droves of horsemen go down the main street. Just then I spotted Rebone tentatively craning her neck on the fringe of the crowd of whites. When I joined her, she told me she had been to the station to see her aunt off to Johannesburg.

'Let's go deeper in,' she said in her usual animated fashion.

'I'm scared.'

'C'mon, Eseki, they won't bite us.'

'We never do it here.'

'But we're already here.' And she pulled me by the arm. It was no use now, we were already inside the crowd. We hadn't been standing long inside there when a huge bony Afrikaner prodded me in the ribs and said, 'Step out, Kaffir! This is no monkey show.'

'We're only looking,' Rebone said.

In a split second I felt a large hand take me by the scruff of the neck and push me out. Another hand from nowhere reached out for me. Another slapped me a few times on the cheek. My face ran into yet another object, so that I felt a sting on the bridge of my nose. I don't know how I was eventually thrust out of the crowd, but I stumbled down the curb. Only then did I feel that someone had kicked me in the back as well. Rebone joined me lower down the street.

We didn't speak for a while. Then, 'The stinking Boers!' she blurted.

'Boer or no Boer, it's your fault.'

'They'd have done it anyhow, wherever we might have been standing.'

'We could run.'

'They like to chase, these people. We'd be *lekker* sport for them.'

It hurt more because she was right. 'What did they do to you?' I asked.

'Just a few hard ones on my cheek.'

'Was Prospect Township like this?'

'They do it differently there. The Police do it for the rest of them.'

'We had no right to go in among that crowd, we shouldn't have gone in.' Tears were gathering in my eyes, and a lump of bitterness stopped in my throat, and I couldn't speak any more. But deep down in the cool depths of this well of bitterness, I felt a strong current of admiration for Rebone. And the cool freshness of it made itself felt deep down in the pit of my stomach.

The Black people conditioned themselves by the day, so as to survive. And the more the white man needed them for his work, the more he hated them. More people poured into Pretoria from the north and the east. The more insecure people felt, the more permanent they looked, as they burrowed into location life, putting up tin shacks on the small plots allowed to the residents. Perpetual refugees seeking life and safety in Jim Crow town.

'Every year the crops grow worse,' some said.

'Our silos are empty,' others said.

'Going back to the country? Madness!' some said.

'Get out of the white man's way!' That is what most of us learned, and learned the hard way. 'The white man's dangerous,' Ma-Lebona would say, after a beer raid. 'And because he's white and can do many things we can't, we think he can protect us.'

'You have seen nothing yet,' said grandmother. 'You should have seen how the Boers protected us in Paul Kruger's day. They did it so well with the gun and the Word of God that the British people couldn't touch us. The white man was your god and what were you to think otherwise? Baas and Missus did your thinking for you. At least you have Marabastad to live in and you don't have to run to another Baas holding a letter in a cleft stick, a letter telling the other Baas to give you a sjambokking.'

Grandmother never tired of telling us about 'Paul Kruger's day'; of the hard times under Boer rule; of the way they buried Africans alive who were suspected of fighting or spying for the British; of how Boer soldiers cut off Black women's breasts; of the hard-hearted 'Meneer Paulen', the German Lutheran missionary who told his flock that God had sent him to drag them out of the darkness which God's curse had hurled them into; of how she excelled in answering Meneer Paulen's scripture questions in church on confirmation day; of how she caused a sensation among the congregation when she answered all Meneer Paulen's questions; of the excitement of confirmation day once a year when candidates dressed in their best and had to prove themselves worthy of confirmation by passing the oral test, knowing also that they would be considered as having 'finished school' after the day, whatever class they might be in at school. She told us of her husband, 'Titus who lies in the grave', the shoe repairer who took his family from place to place looking for a better life; the man with an iron hand and will, very Lutheran, very defiant; the man, as grandmother put it, who didn't think Meneer Paulen better than he.

For Aunt Dora, the past never seemed to hold any romantic memories; she never spoke about the future; she simply grappled with the present.

I often sat on the edge of our back veranda, during my easier moments, and watched Aunt Dora and grandmother bending over their wash tubs. Now bending low to use the washing boards; then standing upright to wash a shirt sleeve or collar; talking away the hours; spitting occasionally into the water; lifting an apron to wipe off the sweat. I watched Aunt Dora, in her thirties: thick-set, with a strong thick arm that seldom missed its target with a bar of soap when she was in a temper.

A number of things sent Aunt Dora into a temper. When tea or sugar was finished in the house and I approached her warily on the delicate subject, she looked daggers at me and then: 'Wasteful, simply wasteful that's the trouble with you and maybe you think I go to the lavatory whenever I want money it's work work work I don't know your wasteful habits are going to strip me naked . . .' And so she rattled on, seeming to have no breath to take until she finished. So, before reporting a catastrophe I waited for a good opening: when she had a visitor who acted as a kind of shock absorber when Aunt Dora decided to rave; or when she was eating meat. She loved meat immensely. More passionately when she was pregnant. She bought beefsteak and put it on the grid over a brazier fire. And then she made herself comfortable and ate with great relish; so that for the few moments when Aunt Dora was in a transport of beefsteak, it sapped her resistance. Then she dug her hand deep into her apron pocket, took out a sixpenny piece and dug it into my palm as if afraid it might slip out. We always bought in small quantities.

Aunt Dora was no dreamer. If she didn't like a thing she paced about in the backyard and denounced it aloud. Unlike my mother, who would come to see grandmother to tell her what she didn't like about Aunt Dora; as when my aunt sometimes used her crockery and cutlery which were stored in boxes in the bedroom; things my mother had collected over several years. Everyone in the family looked up to my mother as the long-suffering patient and wise sister, always ready to help with money and advice. 'Too good for this world,' my aunt said of her. 'I like the person who likes me.' My aunt never wanted a dispute she was involved in to hang, unresolved, for long.

Abdool, the Indian shopkeeper we patronized most, like all other traders, issued small books which he rubber-stamped for every sixpenny purchase. When the book was full with about 200 stamps, it could be exchanged for two cups and saucers. At Christmas, if we produced a book, full or not full, Abdool gave out two cups and saucers and two tumblers for 'Christmas Box'. I bought ten shillings' worth of malt and groceries once, and Abdool wouldn't stamp the book to the full value, saying frankly if one bought so many things, the book would fill up too soon.

Again Aunt Dora towed me behind her, holding the book and me as exhibits for the purpose of righting a wrong immediately, the gravity of which both exhibits were too dumb to appreciate; to right a wrong by rolling someone in the dust a few times and lowering his price on the market, as she said.

'Stamp that book for the ten shillings I bought with, *at once!*' my aunt banged exhibit A on the counter so that pieces of monkey nut shells fell to the floor. 'You say he stamped only for five shillings, eh?' She dragged exhibit B nearer the counter. Exhibit B nodded. She spoke fluent English which she often said she could have improved upon if the death of her father hadn't caused her to leave school.

'No-no-no, a-a-a!' Abdool cried, as if the idea was unthinkable. 'Ten bob too-much-too-much.'

'Abdool, stamp that book before I cause a big smash-up!'

'Dolla-Dolla, *mosadi*, why-for you maker so much *makulu*[1] troble-troble. All-a-time you maker troble-troble why-for?'

'Dolla-Dolla to hell! Trouble comes from you, you cheat. I

[1] Adulterated form of Bantu word meaning *big*.

don't go to the lavatory when I want money see these hands they're rough from work.'

'I holso work for me and my children.'

'Stamp that book I say, coolie! You come from India to make money out of us, eh!'

'Aldight aldight I come from Hindia what he's got to do with book? No-no-no a-a-a!'

'Abdool I don't want any dusty nonsense!'

'If hum coolie ju kaffier ten-times ju-self.'

In a moment Aunt Dora gave exhibit B a hard push away from the counter and reached out for medium-sized Abdool's collar, 'taking him by the laundry' as we called the attack colloquially. The Indian's fez fell off as he tried to jerk himself loose. Aunt Dora placed a heavy knee on the counter. 'Come outside come outside I'll show you what-for you coolie,' she kept saying, and Abdool kept crying, 'Lea' me lea' me kaff'r bitch, Dolla-Dolla!'

She heaved herself and a thick mass of quivering flesh spilt over the counter to the shopkeeper's side. I thought she had broken her neck but she was up in an instant. She propelled Abdool out of the shop and they were out on the veranda. The shopkeeper was spending all his energy trying to wrench himself from Aunt Dora's hold. My heart was beating fast, both from fear and a sense of heroism on the side of Aunt Dora.

Exhibit B was called by name and handed a head kerchief. I immediately thought of exhibit A and two cups and saucers it would soon be worth if Abdool should be vanquished and I made a dash towards the counter to rescue it. I picked it up from the floor and rushed back. A crowd of people had gathered around the two, some jeering, some cheering my aunt, enjoying the fight immensely. Those who seemed to be backing Abdool knew that he was an unwilling horse, but they were having their fun. He was still shouting to my aunt to let go of him.

Within a short time old Elisha, Abdool's bearded father, Abdool's wife, and a crowd of other Indians reputed to be his children, cousins, nephews and nieces and sisters—people we had never seen before, had run out from their living quarters at the back of the shop. They moved about excitedly, adjusting *saris*, clinging to one another all the time, cataracts of Indian words falling from them in a continuous clatter.

Aunt Dora banged her head a few times on Abdool's face as was, and still is, the common technique among fighting women. She drew blood from his mouth. Soon she was on top of Abdool on the concrete floor. They rolled down from the veranda and a few times in the dust, and my aunt, still on top, shouted, 'Are you going to stamp the book, Abdool?' He spluttered a few words and Aunt Dora got up.

Elisha rushed to his son to help him up, and the family were crying openly now and the cataracts of words continued. Abdool looked the sorry sight of depreciation Aunt Dora had set out to prove. She followed the shopkeeper in, adjusting her own blouse which was badly torn, to cover her breasts.

The book was stamped. We almost made the two cups and saucers that day. Aunt Dora got a severe beating from her husband that night, the first and last I ever saw her go through. But she never cried. During the following few days I tried desperately to keep out of range of her missiles.

Grandmother called her a heathen to have done such a thing and said if Titus, now, alas, in his quiet grave, had been living, he'd have blown her head off with his fist like he'd done a few times when she, my aunt, was still a girl. Grandmother prayed for Aunt Dora that night. Trust Dora of Second Avenue to beat up a man, was the general talk in the location.

Some weeks or months after my aunt's assault on Abdool, I was walking from Bantule on an afternoon, where I had been sent, I was feeling tired and I decided to rest on the veranda of Abdool's shop and enjoy the cool shade before I should start on my domestic work. There was something about standing or sitting on the veranda of a shop when you were in your teens. If you were a group you talked about some of the most beautiful things and some of the most sordid things. You laughed in a way that would annoy your grandmother or your aunt or your mother, but you enjoyed the freedom of it. That was where you relived the experience of a motion picture that you had all seen by relating some of its most vivid scenes. You told one another how you hated a particular girl, how you detested a particular teacher, and how you would one night carry a bucket of stools from a lavatory to his classroom and pour the stuff on his table. Alas, but for the smell of it we would have done it! It was on the veranda of a shop that you shared every bit of bread or sweet one of you might have bought. You bought bread and stuffed it with Indian *atcha* and laughed at some passing object with a great deal of impudence. If you were alone, you were in a position to view critically what you considered to be the whole world passing down Barber Street, half-detached, half-committed.

Old Elisha sat perched on a soap box, leaning against the next pillar. His legs were folded in on top there, his sandals lay in front of him below, the inside of them shining. He looked like a magnified trussed chicken at the market. I toyed with the idea of some accident befalling him in that position. Then four boys of the Texas Ranch slouched on to the veranda. They came to stand against the wall opposite Elisha. As far as he was concerned, they might as well not be there. He just kept chewing his nut and releasing a long column of red spit on the ground below him occasionally.

The boys, headed by the pretty-faced Freddie, terror of Fourteenth Avenue, moved about idly, one smoking dagga. Since Boeta Lem—the Blade—had been locked up for rape, Freddie had the habit of moving down towards us, as if he were pushing the borders of his dominion farther east. The other ranches didn't like it of course, and everybody said he was smelling a knife war. There were supposed to be only four boys in the Texas Ranch, with a few unimportant hangers-on and admirers. But they were rumoured to be so powerful that they owned more than half the girls in Marabastad. The bunch of them were most unsecond-avenuish; in dress and everything else. Their trousers came up high to the middle of the legs, and they wore 'white ducks', which were canvas boots. It was also rumoured that the popular local song that was played by brass bands and sung at weddings which went 'White ducks shall never get dirty' had been composed by Freddie.

'Maisie's playing drum,' Freddie said, with a note of triumph. This had become a common expression, after the manner in which the drummer of a brass band carried his instrument on his belly at 'stockfair' parties.

'Who blew her up?' Two asked.

'Guess who?'

'Shishi,' Three volunteered.

'Naw, Shishi couldn't sit on a horse at the merry-go-round,' Freddie said.

'Bombay then,' Four said.

'Talk about somebody better.'

'Elisha,' Two said. The others bawled out with laughter. Two looked sideways at the old man. I felt my bowels shrinking as the Indian turned his head to look at the boys, as if all he had heard was their laughter. Then he looked vacantly ahead of him, again chewing a piece of eternity, his shoes below him, looking as if they might start walking without the owner, right on top of me.

'Who then, tell us, or is it you?'

I thought Freddie would get into a rage. He didn't. 'I go for the tough ones, not Maisie-things. I tackle the tough ones, understand me? Just so they get humble, under my feet I swear by your dad.'

'Ee-jee who?'

'For example, Dunga. Met her at the merry-go-round last night. Hell, outjies,[1] I see her at the fortune-teller's window and I say let's ride the swing, cherry. She turns round 'sthough I was talking to the wind. I go nearer again and I say let's get some ice-cream and then go ride the swing. Know what? The bitch picks up her nose for me, for me, by your ma. I say okay and walk off. Meantime I've two hearts, and one heart says You're coward and the other says Mind the spit on the face. So I say to myself I must leave it for another time. I myself I don't charge like a Pietersburg boxer.'

[1] *Boys*—pronounced *Oakies.*

'And so?' Three asked.

'Wait wait wait, you haven't heard nix. I go to the turnaround swings and there is Dunga just getting on. I jump on to the same one just as the machine begins *te-te-te-te*. She looks scared and opens her eyes as big as two murders. I sit down and put her legs on my laps—'

'What!' Four shouted incredulously.

'By my pa and my ma and your pa and your ma. The swing is flying high now and I say Don't worry, Dunga. I put my hands on her thighs and she looks away.'

'What colour?' That was Two.

'What you mean what colour?'

'What colour did she wear them in?'

'How the bloody hell should I know?'

'Hell, how dirty you outjies can get—sies!' Three said with some concern.

I felt ashamed, scared, incensed all at once and my head was singing a dizzy tune. I looked at Old Elisha. He was still chewing away at eternity, and I was pressing my moist palms against the pillar, wanting to leave and not wanting to leave.

'Since when has your pa been a minister?' Four asked. 'You go on, Freddie.'

'When the swings stop we get down. I hold her hand and hell, she doesn't refuse when I take her out of the grounds to the dark wall back of Tin-my-Moosa's. Now you outjies know how tough Dunga is. Well, no boasting, but we stand there and I kiss her and still no scratching or spitting. I slip my hand in but the bloody watchman comes and drives us off. See what I mean, outjies?'

'Here comes a stuck-up cat,' Two observed.

Rebone walked up the veranda. They whistled. It was just like her to walk in front of hooligans like that. She entered the drapery department of Abdool's shop. When Rebone came out Freddie intercepted her and stood in front of her.

'I fancy you, cherry,' he said.

'Sies, night-soil like you!' She arched her arms at the elbows like a hen that gets ready for an attack.

'No big mouth now, my sister. I fancy you, by your pa.'

Rebone spat into Freddie's face. Elisha looked on abstractedly. I was hot and angry now. The pretty-faced boy took her by the wrist and twisted her arm until Rebone yelled with pain. Freddie brought her to a position where she stood facing him, her breasts heaving up and down against his chest. Her face turned away from his.

'Wipe my face now,' he commanded. 'And clean and pretty as you found it.'

I saw it happen: something about Rebone's carriage sagged. She wiped off her spit with the sleeve of her shirt.

'O.K. I fancy you, remember that, eh?' He let her go. She was drying her eyes with the sleeve of the shirt as she walked away towards Second Avenue.

A woman was coming up at the same time, towards the shop. Gradually it was registering in me that I was going to be under my aunt's nose soon. I jumped up and in running away to disappear round the corner I lost my balance and ran into Old Elisha. All I heard was a thud and the rattling of the box as both fell, and then the cataract of Indian words as they poured out from Old Elisha.

I managed to dodge Aunt Dora that day by the breadth of a hair. She and grandmother had come to loathe boys who hung around on shop verandas.

Sixteen

DINKU DIKAE'S TERROR

'You're coming tonight?' Rebone asked.

'Yes,' I said.

We walked down Barber Street, from school.

'Hai, that new teacher gives too many notes.'

'Well, we're no more in Standard Five, remember.'

'So he must kill us and have no Standard Six any more!'

'I don't mind notes. Makes me feel bigger and still bigger with so many exercise books to carry.'

'Look there!'

'What?'

'My father there in front of Fung Prak's shop. Somebody's stopped him. Let's go and see.'

We found a white man in black uniform talking to Rebone's father, examining the horse as if he were looking for something in the hair, in the mane, under the tail, on the hoofs.

'It's not a policeman, Pa,' I heard Rebone hiss out next to him.

'It's not a policeman, Pa.' Dinku Dikae might as well have been deaf. For the first time I saw a man tremble as the hawker did. He followed the white man round almost falling over him, but not saying a word. Rebone's face was one massive frown, and her attention was on the father all the time.

'Don't be afraid, Pa,' she hissed. 'He's a health inspector, not a policeman.' Of course, he had been stopped several times before by health inspectors.

When the white man left, after saying brusquely, 'All right,' Dinku Dikae held on to the harnessing, like one about to faint.

'Let's go, Pa.' She knew her father wouldn't work for the rest of the day after such an incident. They left Rebone holding the reins. I envied her holding the reins like that, so efficiently.

That afternoon and on into the night the picture of Dinku Dikae, trembling in the presence of the white inspector, could not leave me. Leaning against his strong horse, then moving to lean against the strong wheel and holding on to the spokes that radiated so much strength; then muttering something; then his broad back offset by the wasp-like frame of Rebone as the trolley's wheels gnashed their way down Second Avenue.

Now how come such a strong man with a heavy shoulder should fear a policeman or anybody or anything that suggested a policeman? I felt at once a close alliance with Rebone's father and a little awe for him. Yes, wasn't a policeman made to be feared—his handcuffs, big broad belt, truncheon, his heavy boots, his shining badge? Most of the police, even in our predominantly Sotho territory, were Zulus. They were tall, hefty, with large bellies, vast hips and buttocks and torn ear-lobes. The white police were only to be seen together with Africans when they came in for beer and tax and pass raids. We loved to imitate the Black policemen as they marched up Barber Street, truncheons pointed up, buttocks jutting out as they tried with little success to follow the commander's order, 'Chest out and stomach in!' But we marched far behind them, tremulously.

I went to do school work with Rebone as usual. But the father was sullen and Rebone sad because of it.

'I treat my horse very well,' Dinku Dikae said. 'I treat him very well. What does the white man want now?' He looked at me as if I were involved, the way he was. 'Police police police every time.' He came to sit in front of me, wiping his forehead with the back of the hand. 'I came here for peace and God knows I don't want dust in my path but where's peace to be found here?'

'He's *not* a policeman, Pa.'

'Same to me look at it up or down the street when a white man looks for a fault it is to take you to the police.' He paused.

'She knows it but pretends not to.' He was tacitly ordering me to listen. I did so willingly.

'Let me tell you something, son. We lived in Prospect Township in the Golden City. Three of us, me, Rebone and her mother. If you have never seen Prospect you don't know the world. You must sell beer to live or else work for a white man and why should I work for a white man when God has given me brains to work for myself. I made money enough to wash your body with. God forgive me I don't know but the police can make you wish and do things only the devil wants to do. Rebone's mother, God's woman, she died when Rebone was a child. I ran the long night to a hospital in Johannesburg for a doctor but I came back without a doctor and God be my witness I looked at her mother die, but I don't know how I could not do anything. A woman I called tried her best. She died, with the child, when the night died at one o'clock. I thought these eyes had seen enough darkness in the world until the Government of Johannesburg wanted to take away Prospect and build factories. Our people refused to move and God knows the police came in again and again and again more than ever before to throw out our beer. We cried and carried our arms on our heads and said Government of Johannesburg stop and the white police came again. I don't know but the Government is a strange person. We cried with tears and then we cried with anger and some of us foolish ones God knows I could never do such madness flung stones at the policemen. More of them came and shot bullets at us. A boy hardly your age comes out of the house next to us crying for help and a policeman points a gun his way and kills the child God is my witness while me and Rebone are looking through the window and see the gun smoke and the boy drop dead. Cold. Finished.'

And at the last word the man flung his arms wide which he had been waving about to help along his narrative. Wide with the big tough hands open. So strong, so helpless.

'I wanted to take Rebone here away from Prospect from the Golden City for her to grow up good. I'm from Zeerust in the west in the land of Bafurutse but I don't know I can never go back there again with all the good land gone to the white man but now the famine is here and people don't buy much any more.

There is a little money still only if you don't scratch backward like a hen so you see what you're working for. Now the police again and again and again.'

People said Dinku Dikae was scared of the police because he must have killed somebody sometime in the past. Others said he had a chicken heart. Some said he would just drop dead one day from heart failure.

I wanted to go home immediately, but I was afraid and there was safety in Dinku Dikae's room. We couldn't do any work, Rebone and I, but I couldn't leave. There was a large bed along one wall, evidently the man's, and opposite was a narrower one, for Rebone. There were neat white quilts, the old-fashioned type with triangular patterns and visible cotton strands. A small table and four wooden chairs with high settles and iron wiring and bolts under the seats. Cooking was done outside, as in our home, on a brazier. He kept his vegetables covered with canvas in the trolley, but there were bags of potatoes behind the door. There was one window. A curtain hung on a sagging string in front of Dinku Dikae's bed and was slung up. Above Rebone's bed she pasted on the wall old bioscope placards, one showing Mae West in one of her seductive poses, hovering over the head of Frederic March on another placard. The male stared grimly out of the wall; the female looked like a mermaid that might have been forced to stand on its tail in an attempt to look more human. The placards reinforced my sense of safety. Luckily when I did go out, a bunch of people were leaving a house next to the Reverend M'kondo's, where, I remembered, a choir practice had been going on. A number of them were going my way.

Yes, fewer people were buying the miserable and depressed vegetables Dinku Dikae sold. Rebone left school in January of 1934; in the middle of the Standard Six year, the last primary school year. We were then sixteen. She had to help her father.

'Your father tells me you were at the Columbia last night?' I asked Rebone one Sunday morning.

'What's he telling you that for?' She looked daggers at me.

'They say they'll burn it one of these days so bad it is.'

'What had you gone to do there yourself the other night?'

'Just to look, nothing more.'

'I had a better reason. I was going to dance.'

'Dance?' I gasped.

'Don't girls dance Marabi?' She was looking viciously casual.

'But at the Columbia! Didn't he want to kill you for it?'

'Hmm, he raved and raved and then he took his belt to beat me and I jumped over the table and on a chair, on the bed, and he couldn't get at me. Then he gave up. So funny now I remember it.' She spoke with such animation that I couldn't help but laugh.

Marabastad was ablaze with talk of Rebone's having been to the Columbia. To dance! She even left school for the purpose . . . A girl that was bound to leave school, we knew it . . . She must have been going there long before now . . . Such a humble hardworking papa . . . It's a spear in his heart, this . . . Nurse a nettle and it scratches you in your late years . . . They say he's sickly already . . . It'll kill him, that's what . . . Children of the present generation . . . too clever if you ask me . . . What do you expect in a house without a woman? . . .

Rebone worked hard to help her father. But she went more frequently to the Columbia. 'Business besides!' she said, which was a popular phrase for 'let them mind their own business'.

She tried once or twice to egg me on to the Columbia. I was afraid. I knew I passionately wanted to go; not just to look, but also to dance with her. I dreamt it many nights. But I was afraid. Not simply of my grandmother: I could elude her. Not simply of what people might say: they would never stop saying anything anyhow. I loved Rebone all the more for the strength I did not have. Without even knowing it, I had stopped going to her home.

Moloi, the noisy, spirited boy next door saw it happen and he came and told us about it.

'Ma-Lebona finds her at the water tap. "My child," she says, "daughter of Dinku Dikae, why don't you go back to school?"

' "Why?" Rebone asks her. You should have seen the girl you boys. She looked like our cat before the dog next door.

' "My child," the old lady says, "you're still too young for the whole of Marabastad to say so much evil about you. The things they say you do at the dance hall! They make one freeze with shame."

' "Why don't you talk like this to your children, old mother? You couldn't keep your makoti[1]—two of them, and so you pick on me to give advice."

' "Ao! my own children never spoke to me this way. Ao! my father will rise from his grave God's truth he will."

' "Besides I'm not your child!"

' "Ao! See these grey hairs, child? You'll remember them till you die for insulting each one of them! I'll speak to your father about it."

' "Yes, because you want him to marry you!"

' "Ao, ao, ao, ao, ao!" and the old lady clapped her hands as she spoke, calling Marabastad to come and see a miracle. "You can't repeat those words, child!"

'You won't believe me, boys, but the girl dipped a small dish, small as my hand or yours, into her tin of water and splashed it into the old lady's face.' Then Moloi laughed, and, as was his manner whenever he wanted to enjoy his laughter, pushed me away.

'What did Ma-Lebona say?' I asked.

'Say? You should ask me what she did.'

'Yes?'

'She turned round and left, wiping her face with her clean apron full of pictures of flowers.'

'That wasn't Ma-Lebona!' Danie said.

'Then it was you in women's dress.'

'Ma-Lebona leave like that!' little Links said.

'Want to look for her in the drain then, under the tap?'

'Ag, stop your nonsense talk,' I said, 'I simply don't believe it.'

Tongues got wagging. Rebone had poured water in Ma-Lebona's face. Rebone?—yes. But Ma-Lebona?—no, a fly couldn't sit on her face!

'The little wasp!' Ma-Lebona kept hissing as she told grand-

[1] Daughter-in-law.

mother and Aunt Dora. 'That little wasp will bring home a load in her stomach at her age for poor Dinku Dikae to nurse or she'll drive him to the mad hospital. You hear me, Hibila and Dora, here—' She spat on her hand and pointed her finger to the sky. 'As God's in the heavens I'll bite my elbow if she doesn't get a baby soon.'

'No, don't say that. It's evil,' grandmother said.

'I still say I'll bite my elbow.'

I met Rebone often after that, but neither of us mentioned Ma-Lebona's name. She picked up a lover at the Columbia. It was common talk among the bigger patrons of the place. Fanyan, his name was. From the XY Ranch in Tenth Avenue. A handsome boy whose features cut like a razor-blade. I developed a consuming hatred of the boy. I gloried in the stories people passed round about Fanyan's wickedness. But I didn't have it in me to blame Rebone for her love affair.

Her father clearly didn't like it. His fellow-tenants told us that Fanyan and the Columbia were the cause of the continual use of the whip on Rebone and threats of greater violence from her father.

'Anybody who touches my girl is asking Bantule to invite him.' That was Fanyan's signature tune which passed from tongue to tongue. Bantule was where the cemetery was. Whenever he and Rebone walked down Barber Street the boys in front of Abdool's shop whistled softly into their cupped hands. Fanyan walked like a hero; must have thought himself one.

The liquor squad were often plain-clothes men from the C.I.D., whites and non-whites. They moved together on their raids. The uniformed police, all Africans, were under a white station commander and a few white sergeants. There were only two ways in which one could be escorted by a policeman to the police station. A man was either handcuffed and made to walk alongside a policeman, or handcuffed and walked down to the station by the scruff of the neck. The African police were brutal in their use of the baton. Times without number a man was walked down to the station bleeding like one who had fallen among mad dogs. The stock reply from the police when one wanted to argue against an arrest was: 'You'll explain yourself to the white man,' often to the accompaniment of a clout, a prod with a baton or a cuff with a large paw.

One of the liquor squad, a Black man, was popularly known as Makulu-Skop[1]—Big Skull. His skull was unusually large, like a buffalo's. Grandmother often said, 'Why don't you use the pot that's as big as Makulu-Skop's head?', meaning the largest pot with which it was necessary to cook only once at a time for the family. Soon the pot became known at home as 'makulu-skop'.

Makulu-Skop was a very energetic constable, more so than his white masters. He plundered mercilessly wherever he raided. He would disguise himself as a labourer and enter a house to buy beer. Instead of drinking he would arrest the man or woman of the house. At the mention of his name every drinking party broke up; beer was thrown out through the window; or it was returned to the pit in the yard or under the flooring boards; or poured into a pot on a stove. The name was relayed from house to house.

On a night in the middle of the week, when few people expect a beer raid, Makulu-Skop went round on a lone mission. Three men pounced on him and dragged him, blindfolded, to the plantation at the end of Second Avenue. His body was found hanging from a tree near the sewerage works.

At this very time newspapers were screaming banner headlines, FUSION! FUSION OF TWO POLITICAL PARTIES! GENERAL HERTZOG FORMS GOVERNMENT. The United Party had been born after a mating between two groups of Afrikaner nationalists, the moderate one of which included English-speaking men. Extreme nationalists formed the Opposition. It was all a mystery to me, this whole fusion. But I didn't spend sleepless nights over the matter. I wonder how many people in Marabastad understood the forces at work . . . Cold comfort for the mice that jumped over my head at night or the bugs that feasted on me.

[1] Adulteration of Bantu and Afrikaans: *big head.*

Seventeen

ST. PETER'S SCHOOL

I passed Standard Six in the first class. When I was in Standards Three and Four I envied the boys who were in the lead. It conjured all sorts of pictures of what shape their brains were. Those boys seemed to fetch their honours so effortlessly. And I had to work very very hard in order to pass a test. When I gained a first-class pass I became afraid of myself somewhat. The class teacher presented me with an English book of adventure stories for boys.

Two of my uncles had gone to higher institutions: one to Diocesan Training College (Anglican) in Pietersburg for a three-year teacher's course. He came home twice in the year. His elder brother had gone to St. Peter's Secondary School, run by the Community of the Resurrection. He it was who suggested that my mother send me there, if she could afford it. She earned £3 a month in domestic service, and the fees were £15 a year. Primary schooling also required fees and money for books for my younger brother and sister. Still, she said she would send me to high school. 'You'll come back and be able to look after yourself and the two you're leaving behind.' That's what she said.

Grandmother was most proud about her three sons who had gone to 'college' as she put it. The youngest of them went to a school in Natal for motor mechanics. He was very sorry after the three years there because no garage employs Africans as skilled workers. European trade unions don't allow it, and then the Government does not recognize African apprentices. He is now a bus inspector and does not hope to be anything more. 'You must starve yourself, stinge yourself rice and stew if you want your children to go to college,' grandmother often said, 'and some people don't know it.'

St. Peter's was in Rosettenville, a white suburb south of Johannesburg city. There were only a handful of day scholars from neighbouring mine compounds. Among them about four or five Indian boys came from the city.

The first day I arrived, which was mid-January, I was awed by the solitude and majesty of the school buildings. There was an atmosphere of stability about every brick wall in the place. I felt absolutely lost, although I was with two or three boys from the old Methodist School in Marabastad.

At six o'clock I heard the Priory bell peal with a sound I could never dissociate from the image of St. Peter's in after-years. I wasn't at all pleased at the prospect of sleeping with a crowd of boys in a dormitory. And the wild spirits of what I later got to know as 'Joh'burg boys' rather frightened me. When I woke up in Livingstone dormitory the next morning it was to wrench myself from a dream about a Pietersburg billy-goat with a bell clanging from its neck. The goat's face was transformed into Brother Roger's, the housemaster, who was ringing the rising-bell at one of our windows. I came to think of him and that bell as an institution.

The other dormitories were Grey, Khama, Limbo, Philip and Moffat, holding altogether about two hundred boys, including those of Livingstone.

The classrooms were austere but nothing like our Marabastad shacks. The science laboratory was well equipped.

The boys took turns as dining-hall 'servitors' and also fetched milk from a dairy half a mile away. We also cleaned dormitories and classrooms and kept the grounds in good order. Every Monday the housemaster or the head prefect conducted an inspection of our boxes to see if we had done our washing and ironing properly. Alternately the floors and walls and beds were inspected.

St. Peter's church was one of the most beautiful African churches in the Transvaal Province. It was long and had four chapels on the sides. Domestic workers from Rosettenville and the neighbourhood and residents from nearby mine compounds attended St. Peter's on Sunday afternoons.

Brother Roger was boarding master of St. Peter's. A strict but open-minded man. He caned very hard, I understood; I was happy not to cross his path. He invited several white men to come and lecture to us on various topics. St. Peter's boys and girls were allowed the freedom to debate on any kind of subject. For the first time in my life I felt a sense of release. Brother Roger was always clean-shaven and he never grew his hair long. He moved about with a long light and graceful stride, one hand holding up his cassock and the other hanging mid-air like an actor sweeping on to the stage. He was all energy and vitality, and when he laughed his mirth seemed to sap the blood from his lips and left a tinge of bloodless yellow around them.

'I suppose you think you're marvellous,' he was fond of saying to a boy. Or 'I'll smack your bottom . . . How's the old cow getting on? (meaning my mother) . . . Hullo you crooked old thing! (to annoy the ageing Latin mistress who walked with her head tilted one side) . . . Why can't you stop making that horrid noise, you old geezer? (to the stout lady of St. Agnes's girls' hostel, who coughed so violently in church that she always went into one of the chapels during a service) . . . It's just frightful the way you boys behave when girls enter the hall . . .' His prefects were always right as far as he was concerned.

I hadn't the slightest idea what high school education was for, so for a long time I was bewildered. Mathematics, physics and chemistry were utterly new to me. The First Form boys and girls just grinned and admired the teachers and cuddled in the grandness of the atmosphere—an atmosphere in which pupils ahead of us gloried in chalking out geometry riders and figures on the nearest board they could find. And then they ganged up to watch the heroes solve the riders.

'You'll never be able to do mathematics, my boy,' the African mathematics master often said, exasperated. It pained me because I knew, as much as he was generally acclaimed, that he was an excellent teacher, if rather impetuous. I was easily the best in English and Latin, and managed to keep up a respectability in the first position in mid-year and promotion tests. I discovered I could only understand when I stayed in class after school hours and worked out constructions, riders and equations, slowly, at my own pace. I retained a loathing for arithmetic with all its stocks and shares and dividends and percentages.

For the first time in my life, when I was at St. Peter's, an awareness was creeping into me: an awareness of the white man's ways and aims. There was complete harmony between us and the white teachers at school and between them and the African staff. And yet no one, Brother Roger or the Principal, or the Community fathers, ever said anything about the attitude they thought we should adopt towards whites and white authority outside school. Slowly I realized how I hated the white man outside the walls of St. Peter's.

I had many times before in Pretoria seen tanned Afrikaners supervise African road gangs. A white man stood, with hunched shoulders, hands in the pockets, speaking his instructions with the aid of a trembling index finger. I had taken it for granted that he ought to be there and getting work done by merely pointing a finger. But now when I came upon similar road workers I was filled with impotent anger.

There was a double-decker bus service for Europeans between Rosettenville and the city. Coloured passengers were given a limited corner upstairs. Always. Some white conductors tolerated a few Africans as well. Others didn't. So in most cases we walked the distance or used a most irregular tram service reserved for Africans. A schoolmate and I took a chance on a bus in town to return to school on a Saturday afternoon. We had already gone out of the city when the conductor came. He glowered at us beneath an ungainly cap that couldn't contain his unruly hair.

'What do you want here?' the young bear growled.

'We're going to school,' I said, showing my school pass.

'This is not for Kaffirs.'

'We're Coloureds,' said my mate.

'Black as Kaffirs and you tell me you're Coloureds!' said the young bear. I didn't see any of the European passengers turn to look back. I was struck by their hard backs and hard red necks.

'Step down!' the young bear said, pressing a button near the door.

The bus came to a stop and we stepped down and walked back to school, about four miles. The only thing we ever said to each other, my schoolmate and I, was a long 'Ya!' Every step I took that afternoon seemed to accentuate the pulse of my anger against the whites and my hatred of them.

Sunday afternoon was outing time every week. The head prefect moved with us to the neighbouring hill, and the head prefect of St. Agnes's, the girls' section, brought up the rear with her charge. I was walking with two friends, also Pretorians, along the left curb but on the tarmac. Two whites on a motor cycle came tearing down in the opposite direction. The driver came straight at us and we jumped on to the pavement.

'Voetsek, you Boers!' I shouted impulsively. They turned back. The head prefect came to inquire. They reported the matter to him, and he wouldn't listen to our version.

'Do you want us thrown out by the European people from this place?' the stocky Yorkshire headmaster said to two of us (the other boy had talked himself out of it). 'What? If you're going to swear at Europeans they'll do it, what?'

One of the bigger senior boys called Zephania—known to everyone as 'Zeph'—was the firebrand of the school. He was big and bony and wore large mine boots of which he polished only the bulldog-looking nose. Our uniform consisted of khaki shirts and shorts for daily wear, and he really looked grotesque as he strutted about on the debating platform, predicting doom to South African white rule and British imperialism. 'A nation is no nation without arms' was his popular heroic line. At first it was all a jumble of words to me when political debates went on. Gradually, as I listened, I was beginning to put into their proper places the scattered experiences of my life in Pretoria. Poverty; my mother's resignation; Aunt Dora's toughness; grandmother, whose ways bridged the past with the present, sticking to neither at any one time; police raids; the ten-to-ten curfew bell; encounters with whites; humiliations. But I only succeeded in reconstructing the nightmare which in turn harassed my powers of understanding.

In 1935, the first year at St. Peter's, I had two Coloured friends. Thomas came of an African father from my tribe and a Coloured mother. A lovable and intelligent chum. He had compulsions that made him want desperately to touch everything he passed—a tree, a wall, a desk, somebody's nose. Thomas would stop what he was saying if he thought there was something he had to touch. And then he pressed his finger or the tip of his shoe and looked up as if in a trance, and as if the object he was touching relieved him of a burden. If gutters were charged with electricity we knew it through Thomas and kept clear of such places. He was always talking about a girl of his whose photograph he kept on his person all the time. He swore he was going to marry her. There was nothing uppity about Thomas, nothing like most Johannesburg Coloureds with their superior airs. He always said what made him such a thorough-going optimist was the fact that his upper lip was a little thicker than his lower one, and that the fact that my lower lip was slightly longer than the upper, was responsible for my pessimism.

The other Coloured friend was Peter Abrahams, now a writer of note. I remember him vividly talking about Marcus Garvey, taking it for granted we must know about him. And dreamily he said what a wonderful thing it would be if all the negroes in the world came back to Africa. Abrahams wrote verse in his exercise books and gave them to us to read. I admired them because here was a boy writing something like the collection of English poetry we were learning as a set book in school. I remember now how morose the verse was: straining to justify and glorify the dark complexion with the I'm-black-and-proud-of-it theme.

There was a Jewish couple who lived near the school. The man was stocky and had ginger hair, the woman was full blown in a family way. Somehow Peter made friends with them, and they often came to the school to see him. He glorified in this friendship in a way that puzzled us and filled us with awe. 'He has white friends, you know,' the boys said whenever they talked about Peter. I regarded him as a conqueror. I had a vague feeling that his opinion of Marcus Garvey typified him as someone who was always yearning for far-away places. He used to tell us that he wanted to show the white man that he was equal to him. That frightened me a little and I did not think about it those days.

Peter stayed only a year with us at St. Peter's. But then he had never really been one of us. His name wasn't talked about in the manner in which certain boys' names linger in a school a few years after they have left, like your all-rounder, your sprinter and miler and high jumper and your squire of dames.

It was glorious to find a large quantity of books to burrow into in the school library. For the first time in my life since I met Cervantes, a vigorous figure in tattered garments, during my primary school years, I shook hands with notable men. Men like Robert Lynd, Alpha of the Plough, Addison, Steele, Goldsmith. And then Shakespeare, Dickens, 'Q', R. L. Stevenson. A poem I specially liked to read and commit to memory was Robert Herrick's *To Daffodils*.

We loved to act Form Room plays and funny ones of our own composition. That way I developed a passion for dramatics. I had now outgrown the crude elocution I liked to display on the concert stage in Marabastad in the yelling of Tennyson's 'Huff a leeeeegue, huff a leeeeegue, huff a leeeeegue onwaaaaard' or Byron's *Destruction of Sennacherib's Host*. Again, I didn't have to drink fuel paraffin before a performance, which in those days we believed cleared the throat and reconditioned the vocal cords!

An Englishwoman taught us English and we had a great deal of affection for her. One teacher we did not like was Mrs. Finck, an Afrikaans woman who taught us her mother-tongue as the second official language of the country. She was a tall, wasted woman with long hair on her face. She wore very tight skirts and spoke with an exaggerated guttural accent. Thomas used to say she reminded him of the pillar of salt in the Bible.

When Mrs. Finck came to class and stood there in front of us on her high heels and in tight skirts, we knew she disliked us. She made dainty gestures with her hand, tilted her head one side in sickening mock-coquettish style, adjusted a strand of hair that needed no adjusting—all of which the boys and girls said were pathetically frantic efforts to keep young. She had the habit of pulling up her nose and saying, 'This class smells'. Her stock threat was 'I'll throw you out by the window', which she gave in English. And still we asked one another continually why Mrs. Finck didn't rather teach white children. She left St. Peter's after eighteen months and was soon forgotten.

We had an African arithmetic master we nicknamed 'Six-and-Six'. His jacket was very short, ending at the hips and the sleeves ended far above the wrists. The story went round that he had bought the suit for 6s. 6d. at one of the mine concession stores that sold smelling meat and oily gravy and hunks of bread at one end and clothing at the other.

One of the things we didn't like was Brother Roger's habit of making the whole boys' hostel fast for the whole day and say the Stations of the Cross on a hungry stomach, just because a boy had stolen another's watch or vest and didn't own up!

I joined the Anglican Church with my mother's consent and was later confirmed. I thrilled at the sight of the pomp and regalia and at the smell of the incense on which the service floated. And then those who delivered sermons, the African student priests from the Priory college or the European fathers, didn't shout, like the Methodist or Lutheran or A.M.E. pastors and evangelists. So I was able to surrender myself to the emotional and sensuous intensity of it all.

Even after the first six months at St. Peter's I felt strange back in the streets of Pretoria during the winter vacation. Some of my former schoolmates received me with genuine cheerfulness; others resisted me. But it was such a common thing to go to boarding institutions that on the whole those of us who were lucky enough to go were regarded as little heroes. My sensitivity to conditions had sharpened frightfully. I still helped in cleaning and cooking and carrying washing during vacations until I left high school.

'Wherever have you been all these months?' Ma-Bottles, the alcoholic, asked when I had gone to fetch washing. She was no worse than when I left.

'At school—in Johannesburg, madam.'

'College?'

'Yes, madam.'

She simply snorted and shivered as if to say, 'Well, that's your affair, not mine.'

'That your brother who comes for the washing?'

'Yes, madam.'

'Looks rascally, 'sall I can say. Has the dirty habit of laughing at me.' I took the inevitable shilling and left. The shilling had been going to my brother, in spite of his 'objectionable manners'.

I understood what Ma-Bottles meant about my younger brother, Solomon. His mirth was easily touched off. Especially by other people's disabilities. And then there was an unsettling, when not infuriating, note of derision in his full-throated laugh. 'One of these days your mouth will stay open till you die, my boy, from that laugh of yours,' grandmother often said. And she knew she couldn't do anything about it.

Solomon loved a practical joke. And when he laughed he enjoyed himself immensely: he twisted all over, shook his head violently, shut his eyes tight, swayed about the waist. There was an elderly man who was a friend of the family—Old Vakalisa—he worked at the Native Affairs Department. Solomon went to work under him in the same department during the holidays.

One afternoon Solomon and Old Vakalisa boarded the same bus to go back home. The youngster sat in a row opposite his senior's. At 5.30 the muffled ring of 'something that sounded like a kitchen clock' (as Solomon put it) was heard from Old Vakalisa's quarter. My brother went into fits of laughter. All passengers turned and craned necks to see what the matter was. It turned out that Old Vakalisa's small suitcase was producing the noise. He in turn was chafing in his seat the while, looking helpless and much older, Solomon told us. There were peals of laughter in the bus.

'Why couldn't he open the suitcase and stop the thing?' I wanted to know.

'He had bottles of liquor in the case.'

I had all the while suspected that Solomon knew all about it. He did. Old Vakalisa had bought a clock in town and sent Solomon to put it in the suitcase. My brother found bottles of liquor in it, and hit on an idea: set the clock to alarm when he was sure they would be inside the bus. He would watch the old man to see how he would get out of that one, knowing that if he opened the case somebody would certainly notice the wrapped bottles. African plain-clothes detectives were continually travelling in buses and the old man didn't know who of them was or wasn't in the bus.

'Supposing he'd been arrested!' I gasped.

'What business has an old man like him to be carrying liquor when he knows it's against the law, and he a Black man?'

Still laughing, my brother related how Old Vakalisa had survived the alarm of the clock and come out of it with profuse perspiration on his bald head.

'Tell your mother I don't like your face,' the heavy-bosomed Mrs. Reynecke had said. 'You look too much like a skelm for my liking.' Solomon laughed. It ended our relations with the Afrikaans woman for whom we had done washing for about five years. Mrs. Singer's tea-drinking dog, I was told, had unwittingly been given tea that contained glass particles. They had to kill it. I didn't feel one way or the other about the passing away of the dog. Mr. Goldsmith was as irate as ever. But he didn't show signs that he would depart this world about three months after I had gone back to school.

Rebone was as skittish as ever, more aloof than ever before. She carried on a loose affair with Fanyan now, and it seemed he was just keeping her barely for prestige. Her father was doing very well in his business. So Rebone went back to finish Standard Six.

My mother gave me five shillings for my pocket-money for the next five months.

The year 1936 passed almost uneventfully for me. We didn't go to school on the day King George V died. This was the year Johannesburg celebrated her golden jubilee with the Empire Exhibition. Scholars visited the show grounds, but we were pushed out violently by white hooligans, first from certain departments and then from the grounds.

I still slogged along in mathematics and became one of those who also wrote an examination in it. But I kept on top of the class.

Three important things happened in 1937, in the final Form of the Junior Certificate course.

It was Coronation Year. King George VI was to be crowned. A public holiday was declared. We were offered buns and cold drinks in large 'grandmother cups' with the picture of the King on them. Fifth Form boys decided to boycott the affair and refuse the refreshments. Most of the boys in the school followed their example. We smashed the cups. Word went round that we couldn't with any amount of self-respect accept refreshments on an occasion that wasn't going to bring us the things that we so urgently wanted: more schools, more opportunities for university education; higher wages for our parents; better houses. The school authorities were indifferent and we felt slighted. We tried to feel triumphant about it all and about nothing in particular.

I made love to a girl from Kimberley at St. Agnes's hostel one Sunday morning, our visiting day. After my speedy conquest I didn't feel as triumphant as I'd expected to. The following day, Monday, we met on the square during morning recess in grand orthodox style. I felt the burning strangle-hold of the long grin that stretched from one classroom to another right round the square. I picked up a few stones between my toes not daring to look Maria Louw in the face. I hated the smirk on Thomas's face when he asked me about it all afterwards. 'You need to have your upper lip pulled a little longer, chum,' he said.

I felt hollow and a guilt complex assailed me. 'You must not fail, you must not ever fail an examination, my child.' My mother's words haunted me day and night. My superstitious fear that I'd fail the exams and thereby fail my mother drove me two weeks later to St. Agnes's with a tight-lipped purpose.

'I'm going to leave you. We must part,' I said to Maria, wringing my fingers, for fear of hurting my feelings rather than hers.

'Why, why?'

'I'm busy.'

'Busy people love each other,' she said, naïvely I thought. I shook my head.

'Don't you love me any more?' I wished she didn't look so tragic about it.

'I—I do, of course I do.'

'Have I done anything wrong?' Oh no, not now, not at St. Agnes's—that wounded face, not now!

'No, nothing.'

'Why, then?'

'I've too much work.' If she didn't stop boring into my skin like that I was going to run out with a scream.

'You've another girl!' That did it. Something snapped inside me. But I just sat there beside her, almost insensible. We were quiet for a long time.

'Well, I must go now. Good-bye!'

The hurt accusing look on that tender face flashes back in my mind very often.

Shortly after that I had a nervous breakdown. I lost the half-yearly tests. All the time I thought if I should fail my mother couldn't afford to pay fees for a repeat performance the following year. I recovered and threw myself back into harness.

I obtained a first-class pass in the 1937 final examinations, among three other boys, Thomas included. More than that, I obtained an A mark in mathematics and a B in Latin. I scraped through in arithmetic. 'You need an operation on your upper lip,' Thomas wrote to me. 'Why can't you let yourself go, chum?'

I had my certificate framed and hung it up on the wall. It is still in the same frame, but no longer on the wall.

When we registered for the examination, Thomas gave his surname as 'Bennet', instead of his African one. His reason was that if his certificate bore his real surname he wouldn't be allowed into the Coloured and Indian Normal College for teacher training. And he couldn't think of going to an African school because salaries were abominably low. Which was true. A Coloured and an Indian teacher did not need to have a university degree to get a nice plum teaching job. Those days he was paid four times as much as an African teacher with equivalent qualifications.

I didn't feel let down somehow when Thomas did that. But I didn't wish I could do the same thing. Besides, the attempt seemed too huge for me.

Eighteen

TROUBLE WITH WHITES

What to do? What could I do with a First Class Junior Certificate? Go on to matric? And then? Fort Hare University College? What about the money for it all?

'Have you money to let him take matric?' my uncle who had been to St. Peter's, asked my mother. She looked at him with a strange expression on her face.

'Yes, God will help me find the money.'

'But he must then go to Fort Hare. They don't hire boys with a matric certificate here. They'll simply laugh at him.'

'You know all about these things,' said my mother. 'Tell me what to do; I don't know.'

'Teacher training. That's why I did it. When he's a teacher he can look after himself. That's what I'm doing. The best school is the one I've been attending. Adams College in Natal.'

'Is it Anglican?'

'American Board. They'll take him, don't worry about that. As you've always helped me all my years in school, Sis, I'll show my thanks by paying his train fare to Natal. But it's too late to apply now. He'll have to work till next January, save up for his clothing.'

'Does he want to go to Adams? Do you, Eseki?'

I didn't know what I wanted, so I said yes.

So Adams College it was to be the following year, 1939.

Back in Pretoria I walked the streets looking for a job. I hated every moment of the process for all the humiliation it brought me. I landed a job at last, as a messenger in a lawyer's office. The proprietor was a tall forbidding colossus. A man I never again uttered a 'Good morning' to after trying a few times without success. Maybe it was because his ears were high above me: he never seemed to hear me. Something about him made me think of Scrooge. I trembled all the time I cleaned his ink pots and the large glass on his table. Our eyes never met, so I came to regard him as a machine that generates power but only from somewhere on the fringe of one's awareness.

I ran up and down high buildings where Blacks couldn't use lifts. I made tea and ran errands for the white girls who always seemed to think up something as soon as they saw me. They switched off their dictaphones, took up their handbags, scratched about inside with long red nails and sent me on some private mission, punctuating their instructions with an interminable string of 'you hear? you hear? you hear?' For all this I received £1 a week. My mother kept it all for me, allowing me a shilling a week for the movies. It was a fortune, compared with five shillings for a period of five months at school.

I had my share of trouble with whites and their superior airs. It was, 'yes, John,' here; 'yes, Jim,' there; 'what do you want, boy?' here. I answered rudely where I could have myself heard distinctly. A few times I had white lads chasing me in order to beat me up for 'rudeness' and to 'put the Kaffir in his place'. Luckily they never caught me.

I was restless. My sensitivity was a foe this time. I took offence at the slightest remark from a white man if I vaguely suspected that it was meant for me. I had chronic emotional upsets, so that the more I tried to think things out the faster my spleen seemed to fill up. I woke up nights in a cold sweat; sat up in the dark and tried to remember an unpleasant experience with whites during the day. An eternal dialogue spun around in my mind, in which I imagined the things I should have said to the white man and hadn't had either the chance or the boldness to utter. That girl who phoned an official next door and said in Afrikaans: 'Mr. ——, here's the Kaffir with the documents.' The old man who tottered up to me and said, 'Jim, where's the General Post Office?' The post office clerk who shouted across the counter: 'If you Kaffirs doesn't bloody well stand straight in a line I won't serve you.' One insult after another came back, fresh and poisonous, to plague my sleepless hours. . . .

I continued to go to the local Anglican church. The romance of it didn't matter any more. But I had to keep up a front in grandmother's house. Occasionally, though, the old fire was re-kindled, and I told myself that I belonged to the congregation.

Marabastad life had changed in parts since I left for St. Peter's. Moloi the noisy boy next door and Isaac from Bantule had gone to a teacher training school in the north. Danie, the other noisy boy down the street who liked to imitate Paul Robeson in his boat song in *Sanders of the River*, followed the two later. China, little Links, and the other Foxes, were messengers in town. Siki, the tubercular guitarist, hâd grown much thinner. But Katrina was still in love with him. She worked as a servant in a suburb. A large number of my classmates worked in town as messengers. A number of them had got thoroughly soaked into Marabastad life: the Columbia; Sunday afternoon 'stock-fair' parties where clubs entertained themselves after pooling their wages to give to each member in turns; week-end soccer and tennis, and so on. There was a students' association to which I still belonged. We met every year in the December vacation, to organize a 'daybreak dance' on New Year's Eve and a picnic on January 1st.

Pretoria, like so many other big towns, was alive with political activity. The so-called Hertzog Bills were cause for much bitterness among the Africans. We were given a separate voters' roll; we could only vote communally for white representatives in Parliament and communally for the Native Representative Council (N.R.C.)—a Black Parliament outside Parliament. Once and for all residential segregation was tightened up by law. A Black man could only buy land in 'released areas'. He could not buy land from a white man and vice versa.

Some of the big men in African politics weakened to the lure of a representative council. The bunch that went to see Hertzog about the Bills split on the issue. Those who are interested in the development of non-white resistance movements are still debating the question: who broke away from whom, and who sold out, between the African National Congress and the All-African Convention.

In 1938, when I worked in Pretoria, it was a common thing to see political meetings on Sundays under the banner of the African National Congress (ANC). I attended out of sheer curiosity and never really followed what was going on. Even before I went to high school, a young man called Tekane from Fifth Avenue used to move about talking politics endlessly. We thought he was insane, because he often broke into a 'secret session' of the Foxes and told us how evil the white man was, and said much else that we knew and felt every day. The birth of an ANC branch in Pretoria seemed to provide Tekane with a chance for useful but confused activity. Some of the older people said they didn't think his father should have tried to send him to Fort Hare University College: the reading of such big books as he often talked about had given birth to a worm which was wriggling in his head to find an exit—so they said. Tekane's father had thrown in the towel when his son was doing second year in Arts. He couldn't afford the fees. So Tekane had come back. He mixed his political talk with religious proclamations and prophecies. The day would come for the white man to do the same dirty work as we were doing, earn their money the way we were earning it, live in Marabastad and enjoy the smell from the sewage works. We would move up to take the white man's place. God had willed it that way.

In the winter of 1938 Tekane committed suicide by hanging himself on a tree in the bluegum plantation. An official of the National Congress, was a tall, hungry-looking gentleman with an eagle nose and protruding cheek-bones. He sold meat in the location for a living. Then he fell ill. As he was getting worse, the story went that he had embezzled Congress funds. Money was certainly missing. The officials all pointed fingers at him. Then the oral bulletin reported that he was dying. But his heart couldn't stop beating because, as he himself shouted to those around him, he was burning in the flaming paper money he had taken. After constant prayers around his bed, he left us to face the Hertzog Bills.

I took courage in my own hands and told Rebone how much I loved her. That was on a Sunday evening, just after witnessing another of the savage *malaita* stampedes. A white constable had run down one man on his horse. Unlike in the days when we enjoyed chasing after *malaita*, I was upset. So when I went to Rebone, it was also to seek a cushion to absorb the shafts that tormented my life.

She laughed. 'You can't be serious, Es'ki?'

'How would you like me to show I'm serious?'

She paused.

'Let's not be.'

'But I am.'

She laughed. The natural deep tone in her laughter was too near the truth of what I feared she felt about me. I couldn't suppress a feeling of annoyance.

'What about Fanyan?' she said suddenly.

'Now you can't be serious.'

'Let's forget the subject. Tell me, what's playing at the Empire?' The Star Picture Palace had been rechristened.

I told her that with Fanyan's shadow hovering between us I didn't dare ask her to the cinema, much as I wanted to. Grandmother now allowed me more freedom to go out at night, as long as I reported to her where I was going and it wasn't a fantastic request I was making.

Sunday night. A stupor settled over Marabastad. At this time, a man might stagger and sway down Second Avenue, singing raucously. From somewhere in the location brass band music would still be blaring away at some party. The week-end was closing up. The last few hours of a violent week-end life were running out. Tomorrow: working day. The last customer left our house, brandishing a trotter in his hand which my brother had gone to buy for him. But first, the man staggered to the back of the lavatory, leaned against the wall, rested his head on his bent arm, looking up into the sky occasionally. He seemed to be alternately switching on and switching off some mechanism inside him that regulated his attention to the urine he was letting out. The next day, I knew, my brother would be pulling a long lip as he tried to clean up the stinking mess in the lavatory. Sounds of yelling and screaming still floated across to Second Avenue from the heart of the location; a heart beating feebly but reminding one of the lusty life it had shared and given since Friday night.

I had left Rebone's about three hours before. Suddenly she came to our home, most agitated. She went to grandmother.

'He has killed him, the constable,' Rebone was saying.

'Who?' Aunt Dora asked.

'Papa. Papa has killed a white man, a policeman. Dead. He's lying dead on the floor.'

'Come, child, let's go,' grandmother said, fetching her black shawl. Aunt Dora and two uncles followed.

Rebone told me all about it the next day. And she later gave exactly the same evidence in court at the trial of her father. The story went something like this:

We are sleeping, pa on that side of the room and me this side. Pa is very tired, he is sleeping like a dead man. He left his food on the table. He eats very well but he didn't touch the food so I leave it there for him to eat when he wakes up at night. I haven't shut my eyes and I hear a knock at the door. I ask who? I'm a policeman, open! And his voice sounds rough and angry. I say I'm afraid it may be a crook, how can I know? Open, Kaffir, he shouts. I know he must be a white man and must be a policeman, but I wake up pa, afraid he'll eat me up for waking him. I tell him a white policeman is at the door. He sits up on the bed and rubs his eyes. He says, What? I say, Policeman, white. I go to the door and tell the man pa is coming to open. I look at pa and pa's face is angry. He's trembling again, he always trembles when he sees a policeman. The white man comes in alone with a big dazzling badge on his hat. Why do you let me wait outside so long, he says to pa. Eh, Kaffir—what are you hiding? Nothing, pa answers and it's the last word he ever spoke. You lie in your big black mouth or else you were busy with your bitch here in the blankets, meaning me because he points at me. Quickly my father stops trembling like I've never seen him. The white man goes to pa's bed and pulls off the mattress and bedding, looking for I don't know what, but I think European liquor. He curses and curses and comes to my bed. As he's bending over it pa, not trembling any more now, takes the bread knife from the table and goes to the bending white man. The white man lifts his head to look at pa, and pa drives the knife deep into his neck on the side. Pa leaves it there and the policeman drops on the floor kicking and kicking and jerking while pa looks at him and says I'll never be afraid of a policeman again, God's my witness if my name is Dinku Dikae!

Rebone later told me Dinku Dikae had said to her she should hide nothing, she must tell the whole truth. And when she did so in the witness box in court, for the first time I saw her sob. She looked terribly frail.

All Dinku Dikae ever said in his own defence was, 'I killed him, he insulted me and everyone who carries my blood in their veins.' And then he told the court what the policeman had said to him. Otherwise the prisoner refused to answer any questions.

He was sentenced to death. I remember feeling how strong and pure his body looked as he was led out of the court by the police. I saw him again a few days before I left Pretoria. He looked more composed, stronger and surer than I had ever seen him.

My two uncles were teaching locally. The youngest of them was still in the school of motor mechanics. My younger brother, Solomon and my sister, Tabitha, did most of the housework I used to do. Aunt Dora was as fiery and robust as ever. She still said often: I like the person who likes me, and she still loved meat. Grandmother, now over sixty, still helped Aunt Dora do suburban washing. She was looking much graver, and still swore by 'Old Titus in his grave'. The day Dinku Dikae was sentenced to the gallows, utter gloom fell not only on Second Avenue but on Marabastad, as a whole and on Bantule, Cape Location and spread to Lady Selborne. I didn't hear grandmother say, 'Death for death—that was Paul Kruger's law.'

During 1938 I felt poverty crawl all over me in a way I hadn't done before. It wasn't just a state I had been born into. That was the year I aimed at buying a suit for the first time, which I could use on Sundays at college. I dropped fifteen shillings at the tailor each month for ten months. Yet I couldn't raid garbage tins in Indian backyards any more.

Later in the year I went to work as a messenger in the Department of Native Affairs at £5 a month. I carried files from one office to another and made tea and ran errands for the typists. I had a few moments in between, during which I waited for a buzz in the small room where I made tea. I read R. L. Stevenson's *Black Arrow*, Dickens's *A Tale of Two Cities* and something by Scott. I did some other reading at home. There was a tall, thick-set lady typist who supervised my tea-making. She was incessantly knitting and she made me think of Madam Defarge very much. She had the habit of offering me sandwiches she had bitten into, and I refused at every instance. Yet she continued to give them to me with unbeatable inanity.

When I told grandmother about it she complimented me on it. 'Shows you have our blood in you,' she said with tight-jawed grimness, as if I had made the right choice by having her blood. She made a great deal of fuss about her tea, and how it had to be made. Once a white woman she washed for in the suburbs on two days in the week sent her tea in a mug. She refused it. After that she always carried to the suburbs a tiny teapot, a spoonful of tea-leaves, a little sugar, a cup and saucer, and a tin of condensed milk in her basket. 'I told her to give her grandmother tea in a mug, not me.'

I wondered a great deal about grandmother those days. Product of Berlin Lutheran missionary teaching with its rigid discipline; the teaching that broke down a good deal of the individualism of the eastern Transvaal Africans and made them grovel on their stomachs for what crumbs the white man allowed them in their slummy semi-rural locations; the product of Pastor Paulen's disciplinary code under which he pronounced damnation from his *preekstoel*—pulpit—for sinners, and cut off some from the church, and suspended others and forgave some. And yet, while grandmother gave in on certain things, she fought like a cat to defend her individualism where the white man was not armed with a bandolier of laws.

Just before I left for the school in Natal, Fanyan disappeared. Rebone showed me a number of papers on which her father had kept a record of his money, his transactions, his Post Office savings. The handwriting was bold and showed some of the largeness of the man who had written it. He had, after all, profited by his daughter's teaching. He had saved up a considerable amount of money. He had asked Rebone if she wouldn't like to go to school for teacher training. She jumped at it and went to Kilnerton Training Institution, a Methodist school in the district of Pretoria. This was after she had sold her father's business and other possessions. She handed the money over to the authorities of the school to keep it in trust.

We wrote to each other often, and as often she warned me against the passion with which my letters were written. They just barely passed through the censoring fingers of their matron!

Nineteen

ADAMS COLLEGE

We arrived at Amanzimtoti (sweet waters) by taxi, twenty-two miles out of Durban. Then we walked a few hundred yards, and plunged into a new world: Adams College—A-DUMS COL-LEGE, as the Zulus pronounced the name. A human jungle of about 400 men and women, double the population of St. Peter's and St. Agnes's together. This then 80-year-old American Board of Missions foundation sprawled over a large area of land. We travelled long distances between Jubilee, the men's hostel, and the classrooms and chapel and dining-hall. When the students poured down from Jubilee, they were like a stampeding herd. I soon got used to hearing boys shout or chant Zulu war songs from a balcony. Both the men and the women were generally big, tall, bony people, unlike the bunch of us detribalized and sophisticated up-country folk.

The first thing that struck me when I arrived were the massive buildings of stone blocks, the violent growth of vegetation around, and dormitories that could easily have accommodated a fair-sized gymnastic club. The floors were always dusty and the inside of these miniature halls smelled strongly of semi-dry grass, which was used for stuffing mattresses. Those of us who had come out of St. Peter's immediately realized that it was going to be impossible to uphold our former standard of cleanliness. There was no inspection of dormitories and boxes at Adams. None of the scholastic aura St. Peter's boasted. Adams was more like a mine compound.

Dr. Edgar Brookes was principal of the school, and under him were headmasters in the high school, teacher training, industrial and music departments. He was a Senator representing Natal

Africans in the Upper House of the Union Parliament. A stockily-built man with a large professorial head and a timid upper lip and soft watery eyes that looked wounded and apologetic. He had been a professor of political science at the Afrikaans University of Pretoria.

The doctor was away in Cape Town during parliamentary sessions from January to June each year, rushing back for the brief Easter recess. When he was away a small beaver-like German, Dr. Brueckner, acted as principal: a philosopher, theologian, electrical engineer, builder all in one. He had a small goatee and was always dashing about like a squirrel preparing its winter store. He was most unpopular with us because of his brusqueness, while most of us had a wholesome respect for his superior.

There was a strange assortment of African and European teachers at Adams: tired-looking, bored men; retired, decrepit, cantankerous white professors one has come to associate with mission institutions; very large African teachers, one with a smile as broad and unfriendly as the ocean; grim-looking white missionaries who were always telling us at speech day how lucky we were to receive an education.

The house-master was a bloated little Zulu with a walrus moustache. He was nicknamed *Sakabula* (a bird that feeds on guavas, which were full on the campus). He always blew the after-meal whistle with food in his mouth. A pure sound was quickly followed by a sharp high note. His voice, eyes, moustache, and broad belt that dropped below the tummy in a vain attempt to negotiate the bulge, were always sagging.

Dr. Brookes set up a sons-of-chiefs' course. This was based on his belief that government institutions like chiefs, local councils, advisory boards, Native Representative Council, which were specially for Africans, could be used profitably in the training of our people in the processes of democracy. It all came out in the civics course he conducted in the school when he was home.

But we didn't enjoy freedom of expression as at St. Peter's. Zeph, the one who used to wear mine boots at St. Peter's was also at Adams at this time, taking a post-matriculation teacher's course.

He still had his old fire, but he felt closed in and most restless. The result was that he and three of his colleagues openly defied authority by sitting on chairs meant for European members of staff at a concert in the school hall. They did so because, as they put it, they didn't see why Europeans should have reserved seats. Actually, it turned out that the seats had been put aside for any member of the staff. The four of them were expelled. They were later readmitted on condition that they serve their punishment by carting soil in wheelbarrows for more than a week.

I always felt as if I were going to be crushed under the feet of so many men and women. In such an ascetic American Board Mission atmosphere one had to thrive on very long journeys to outlandish schools for teaching practice.

The following year the boys struck because we believed we had been given meat from a cow that had died from some disease. The ringleaders were expelled. We came to accept it as a stock technique the white man was always going to use whenever non-whites under him agitated for certain things. Whenever students from various mission institutions met and compared notes we found the same method had been used in several other schools: find out the ringleader and sack him.

Just about this time the country developed a rash of school strikes. Fort Hare University College featured in the events of the time. A vigorous group of young men was in the making, with a sharp political consciousness. This was later to find an outlet through two political camps: one, the nationalist Youth League of the African National Congress; the other, the not-so-popular but highly intellectual flank of the All-African Convention.

The more intense political feeling became at Fort Hare, the more intractable and ruthless the missionary authorities became. In a great number of their schools (the Government only began to establish day high schools in 1940 in drips and drops), certain political journals were banned; topics for school debates were severely censored, so that political discussions became taboo; pupils expelled from one school had not the slightest chance of entering another. As the world war raged on, the temper of the students raged to the extent that certain school buildings were burnt down. Nor did the end of the war have any pacifying influence. Five years after the event school buildings were still going up in fires. One Lutheran missionary institution improvised prison cells for offenders. Adams College itself lost its beautiful high school and library buildings: they were gutted by fire. Church and missionary leaders shrugged their shoulders and said:' They're cutting off their noses to spite their faces . . . it's foolish . . . they must take the consequences. . . .'

My own political consciousness was vague—in an intellectual sense. I shut everything out of my life practically. I mustn't fail, I mustn't fail. The spectre came back to haunt me. Then a miracle happened. In the second year I was told that the Natal Provincial Education Department had granted me a scholarship to cover my training fees for the two years. This was done on the strength of my first-class pass in the Junior Certificate examinations. The money my mother had slaved so much to pay, excluding the money for books, was paid back to her. About £22. The reply I received to my letter about this was soaking wet with tears. She used £15 of the money to sue for divorce—nine years after my father had left us. She went through the case smoothly, because my father had already married by customary rites and had three children by the second wife.

I left Adams with a nagging memory of the strong spirit of tribalism that prevailed in Natal. Natal had two tribalisms: the English and the Zulu brands, with the Indian at the butt-end of both. The province is predominantly Zulu country, and the bulk of the students at Adams have always been Zulus. They did not like non-Zulu boys and girls coming to the college. They regarded us as foreigners, to be avoided. They regarded us from the Transvaal as dangerous rascals and they had the superstitious belief that we carried deadly knives in our pockets.

Towards the end of 1940, someone from a Reef town wrote to the principal of Adams College asking if he could recommend a student due to leave college who might want to work in an institution for the blind as a clerk. The headmaster of the teacher training department put the proposition to me. I was intrigued by it. I don't know what it was that attracted me towards the work, because I had always passionately wanted to be a teacher.

I do know that I felt unsure of myself. My personality was simply a whirlpool of currents and cross-currents of ambition and idealism mixed up with memories of my home life. I had seldom thought about my father, but when my mother sued for divorce it seemed old wounds had revived. The smell of paraffin gas from a pressure stove; the smell of boiling potatoes and meat and gravy and curry; the sound of my mother's screaming; the smell of hospital chemicals and bandages; the sight of a man with a brutal limp. . . . Sensations that had lain dormant for nine years, why were they rekindled? 'You must go on calling yourselves by his name, my children,' mother said, 'it won't take you away from me ever.' We kept the surname. Suddenly I felt as if my life had been one huge broken purpose.

So in a moment of reckless abandon I went to 'Ezenzeleni', the only institution for the care of African blind in the area covered by the Transvaal, the Orange Free State and Natal. The man who had written to Adams was the Rev. Arthur William Blaxall (now Doctor), then superintendent and secretary. I remember vividly now the afternoon he fetched me by van from Roodepoort station, twelve miles out of Johannesburg, in January of 1941. I was twenty-two, a great deal confused, utterly unsure of myself, but feeling a kind of inevitability as I entered the service of Ezenzeleni.

I was given an hour a day to teach myself touch-typing from a manual. The clerical work was pretty light, but I did several other things in between. After learning driving from Mr. Blaxall over about two months, I delivered blind-made goods in suburban Johannesburg and nearby towns. I carried baskets, mattresses—some clean and some smelling of ancient urine—in and out of the van. I collected mail in the mornings by van. Twice a week I taught a few literate blind men how to type, a job I enjoyed immensely. I was paid £6 10s. a month—what I would be earning if I were a full-time teacher. I paid £1 towards my monthly board and did some extra-mural work in lieu of rent and the rest of my board. One Sunday in the month I took the blind men and women to church in the location about half a mile away. I continued to attend the Anglican church in the location and morning Mass in the institution chapel, which Mr. Blaxall conducted. Again, with a sense of inevitability.

That very year I began private studies for the Matriculation certificate. It was hard, having to buy books and send money to my mother and clothe myself. During the four and a half years I worked at Ezenzeleni I never saved a shilling. It was while I studied for the Matriculation that the institution found it necessary to reorganize its accommodation. I had to look after a batch of blind men in a house in the slummy and rusty location. I had a room to myself. The blind men came to call the house 'Silver House' because the corrugated-iron walls and roof had new silver paint on. They continued to call it so even when, later, I told them it had been repainted green. 'If it bothers your eyes, it doesn't bother ours,' Meshack said simply. He was the man at whose wedding with a sighted schoolmistress I was later to act as best man. The men conducted themselves most admirably, while at the same time they worked themselves into the social life of the location, such as there was. I had very few such contacts myself, engrossed as I was in my studies, varied only by night screams and drums and the blaring of amplifiers and the half-pagan, half-Christian singing of the Zionist sect. After eighteen months we went back to the institution grounds, because the owner of Silver House was taking it back. The second year I wrote six subjects for the examination under the Joint Matriculation Board of the University of South Africa, an establishment which has always catered for external students, equally for Europeans and non-Europeans. I passed the examination in the third class and felt most disheartened. The superintendent urged that I be paid £10 a month plus a cost of living allowance of about £2. I couldn't hope to be paid more, I was told, because his management committee felt that the job I was doing didn't warrant higher qualifications than the junior certificate or teacher's certificate. In the meantime I had taught myself the Pitman system of shorthand, and was taking dictation proficiently.

Still I couldn't save. My brother and sister were in a day high school in Pretoria, and family demands were growing. I asked myself naïvely several times if Hitler couldn't have foreseen that his war was going to strangle some of us who had known only stinking poverty since we were born.

I struck a warm friendship with some of the blind. Velile, the evangelist, who later married a semi-blind woman from the Ezenzeleni women's hostel; Meshack the tiny man with an intelligent face; Adam Daniels, the Coloured man, who came once a week from a Coloured township in Johannesburg to learn typing. He was learning the saxophone also.

I spent my vacations in Pretoria. Soon Marabastad was to move. The location on the other side of the river had already dissolved. The Berlin Lutheran Mission there had collected money from the residents to buy the piece of land adjoining the poor white section of the town and cut off from Marabastad by the river. The residents built their mud shanties on small plots allotted to them. It was several years later when the whites decided they didn't like Black people so near them. The municipality had been petitioned to remove the location. It didn't occur to any of the higher-ups that the residents would have to move to *some* place else. The 5,000 or so people scattered, but not before they tried to claim from the Mission the money they had collected. The Mission had received a large sum as compensation. Their efforts failed. They either hadn't been given receipts or had all lost them. The site was converted into a Rugby field for whites and later into a municipal bus depot.

This time the municipality itself took the initiative with the approval of the Smuts government, to move Marabastad to Atteridgeville, nine miles out of town. Several tenants were happy enough to be able to live in a three-roomed house with electric lighting, sewerage lavatory, a small coal stove and fenced yard, away from the squalor of Marabastad, although the rooms were ten feet by ten. Those who owned houses in Marabastad were most grieved because compensation was utterly low. Also, they hadn't been consulted, and they had owned their houses, which they wouldn't be allowed to do in the new location. Tenants and landlords both complained about the distance they would have to travel to and from work, using very bad wartime bus transport. The lengthening bus queues were doing the people's tempers no good.

Grandmother resigned herself to the change. 'That's the white man's law,' she mumbled. 'It will be nice living and dying in a new fresh house. I don't know it will be hard losing so much money on this house but wherever I go I want my dead body laid beside my man at Bantule. The white man is our god now what can we do and I can only be happy to know I have sent you all to school and you can look after yourself wherever you go so God's shadow will always be beside you.'

House, No. 2A Second Avenue, came down. I believe the mice scattered. Grandmother's last-born had saved up enough money as a bus driver to place a deposit on a stand with an old house on it in the African freehold township of Lady Selborne, ten miles out of town. He took grandmother with him. Aunt Dora and her family also bought a stand and house in the same township. My two other uncles went to teach on the Reef.

My mother had to leave domestic service in order to look after her two other children in her new house in Atteridgeville. She took up a job at the city's mint and travelled up and down daily.

She was showing signs of thinning. She was as hard-working as ever—she had the reputation for industriousness as well as infinite patience inside and outside the family. 'Deadly patience' Aunt Dora continued to say accusingly. My mother nearly broke down completely when my brother and sister both decided that they were not going to high school any more. They didn't see the point of it, they argued, and they knew I could never afford to send them both to training colleges. She consulted me about everything and I felt ashamed whenever I failed to live up to her expectations, whatever they were. We had been living apart all those years, and now that I could be close to her during every year, and certain week-ends, my mother overwhelmed me so much that I felt most bitter over my inability to thank her substantially for all she had done for me and the others. Her abundant love sometimes made me wish we could quarrel. Meantime, I noticed her strength was flagging.

I often visited Rebone during the vacations. She was now teaching in Marabastad, the section which took the municipality over three years to clear completely. She was a tenant in this section.

We talked over our earlier years in a stupid adult fashion: the Methodist School, now a ghost of what it had been, making me feel a little ashamed of taking such a mean advantage of revisiting it during a hard time; stolen nights at the Columbia; Fanyan; Abdool, who had sold his shop to another Indian who must have been much more optimistic; many other people except her father. Rebone had even more dignity about her carriage, but she was still wilful. I asked her once more if she found it impossible to love me as I loved her.

'We're still brother and sister, Es'ki. We grew up together, we know each other too much, how can we be lovers?'

'You didn't like my letters when you were at Kilnerton, then?'

'That's not the point at the moment.'

Shortly I heard at Ezenzeleni that Rebone was involved in a romance with an Indian doctor. I was told it was the talk of almost the whole of Pretoria. 'What don't we have that the Indians have?' some said. 'Money,' others said sarcastically. I had to swallow a good deal of my own indignation. But I never thought of her as being in love with an *Indian*; mine was just basic jealousy. 'She can't be African as she says,' some people summed up, 'she's Indian blood for sure . . . We weren't born yesterday, you know.' To all this Rebone didn't seem to give a twitch of a hair.

When I saw her lover, I concluded that he was just the sort that would burst through the barricade of convention to fall in love with an African. He had a dashing, eager pirate's look, a very dark, shining moustache, deep glistening eyes. He looked keyed up all the time. A few months later he was killed in a motor-car accident. Rebone, who had been with him, escaped death by the breadth of a hair.

I was called urgently to Pretoria in the autumn of 1943 because my mother had had a stroke. I found she had been rushed to hospital, where her case was diagnosed as sugar diabetes. I also discovered for the first time that she had been feeling some illness coming for a long time, but couldn't think of leaving work. She had to, this time, and she was given medicine to inject herself with.

A group of singers came from a teacher training institution to entertain the blind at one time. Among them was a young woman, my age, who recited something from Wordsworth to the audience. Something happened and within a short time I had arranged to visit her in Sophiatown when she would be home during the nearing school vacations. It was her final year at college. I surprised myself with my conquest, because in a few moments a pact was made between me and Rebecca. Her father had died and she lived with her mother in a tin shack in Sophiatown. Her father had left them a stand with some rooms to hire out. But they had a heavy bond on the property for a four-roomed building they had just put up. Evidently, the two had known little, if any, luxury. Rebecca was born in Vrededorp, a dirty old slum township nearer Johannesburg city. Her mother, like mine had done when I was still in primary school, brewed beer and sold it. Later she gave it up. The police always win in the end. Few, if any, women are known to have continued selling illicit beer until late in their fifties.

When I wrote and told Thomas about my affair with Rebecca he passed over his Rosicrucian blah-blah once more about long thick and short thin lips.

A few days later I was baffled by a long long letter from Rebone telling me how passionately she loved me; that she had known it all the time; that she couldn't face a love affair with someone she had got so used to as a school- and playmate. I remembered then that Rebone, like me, was a cinema fan. I couldn't fall back on my pact with Rebecca; I didn't really want to. No, I couldn't retrace my steps, even for the sheer exercise of it! Still, I knew it wasn't going to be easy driving Rebone out of my thoughts. I didn't try. When I met her later, she said: 'I suppose you've found somebody better among the Reef girls, have you—those very smart girls?' In a sense, she was right, because I had found someone who had responded to my love much sooner and more generously. But I never blamed Rebone, really. She later married a teacher, and seemed tolerably happy. To this day, she remains a lingering memory of what might have been, which memory serves as an ornamental lace to what it is; like the lace of a petticoat which is all right as long as it doesn't show.

My years at Ezenzeleni gave me a stability of purpose. I had sufficient time to turn inside out, to live with my windows open, as it were. I unwrapped myself. Seeing the blind consciously groping about for a purpose and creating for themselves a spot of cheerfulness did it. The sight of poverty always aroused in me the most violent feelings. Some of the blind men and women had been found in derelict circumstances. I learned to see my own poverty against the bigger canvas of non-white suffering.

An African social worker, Alfred, came to join me in my room. He worked for the Deaf and Dumb Association, of which Arthur Blaxall was the chairman. Alfred had epilepsy. Several nights, especially when it was full moon, he woke me up with a sharp scream and the creaking of his bed as he shook in a fit of convulsions. I quickly got up and inserted a spoon in between his teeth. The following morning he could never get up, from sheer physical weakness and a feeling of shame; then his face looked like raw leather. He was a most cheerful cynic. He had a frank face and a candid if often upsetting manner of speech. 'Why tell *me*?' he would say to someone who tried to confide in him. 'Would you say the same thing you want to tell me in the presence of the man you're going to speak about?' 'I don't see why a man should pick on *me* for his audience—I can't think he has healthy motives. . . .' That characterized Alfred's relations with people. The only thing on which Alfred and I could exchange confidences was the subject of oppression and the unreliability of whites. We had some of the most bitter things to say to each other about white missionaries in the schools we had attended.

But his fits caused him great anxiety. He never complained though. During the two and a half years I lived with him I got a glimpse of that something in human suffering which I had never experienced before. Thirteen years later, in 1957, Alfred was murdered in an eastern Reef town in most mysterious and ugly circumstances which suggested ritual killing.

It was on a June night in 1945 when I sat up, keeping watch over Alfred, who was just dozing off after a fit. During the day I had decided to leave Ezenzeleni, to enter my profession. I felt I wanted more room to fly. That was when I had received a letter from the principal of Orlando High School, the only secondary school serving more than 100,000 residents in Orlando. I was being asked to join his staff as Afrikaans and English master. That night I wrote a letter to Arthur to tell him my decision.

Rebecca and I had arranged to be married on 29th August 1945, which would be just after I should have started at the school. My mother was very pleased and looked the happiest woman alive. She sent out her invitations and marshalled her friends and relatives who would help prepare the wedding feast. After the African fashion, the first feast would be at the bride's home and the second at the groom's. I went to see her on a week-end to get a few utensils for use in my Orlando house. I found she had had an attack and was in bed. She didn't speak much, except to say, 'I feel very, very tired, like I'd been walking miles and miles.'

After a week, it turned out that I had seen and heard my mother speak for the last time that day I left her in bed. I received a telephone call to say that she had passed away, in grandmother's arms. A diabetic coma had done it. She was forty-five. In the train to Pretoria the thought kept tormenting me: why did you have to leave at this time, mother—just when I was bringing a bride home to make your heart glad, why, why? It came again and again while the wheels of the electric train babbled like a laughing idiot as they ground the miles. We buried her on the king's birthday.

Grandmother went to live with my brother and sister, who were working in Pretoria.

Interlude

Marabastad is gone but there will always be Marabastads that will be going until the screw of the vice breaks. Too late maybe, but never too soon. And the Black man keeps moving on, as he has always done the last three centuries, moving with baggage and all, for ever tramping with bent backs to give way for the one who says he is stronger. The Black dances and sings less and less, turning his back on the past and facing the misty horizons, moving in a stream that is dammed in shifting catchments. They yell into his ears all the time: move nigger or be fenced in but move anyhow. They call it slum clearance instead of conscience clearance—to fulfil a pact with conscience which says: never be at rest as long as the Black man's giant shadow continues to fall on your house. Before the house came down in which he had hired a room, Siki the tubercular guitarist, coughed, as Old Remetse said, like the twang of his guitar strings, and coughed and coughed until the blood came out and he died. Many Sikis will be born yet but few will die the way he did with his fingers entangled in the broken strings of his instrument. Some say they heard him that last time. Katrina, his eternal lover who paid his rent, wept sorely for him and grandmother said that Siki had gone to the place where no rent is asked for and where they would give him many more guitars to play to God. Rebone left us too, after mother. A mysterious disease swept her off in a whirlwind. I know now she loved me and wanted me more than I imagined and that her married life was—what does it matter now? Like her father she had lived lustily. Ma-Lebona has gone my son, grandmother told me, Ma-Lebona has gone: remember the one who lived opposite us in Second Avenue and failed to rear husbands and daughters-in-law, the mother of that goat called Joel who still sucked from his mother until her death weaned him.

Interlude

Grandmother said Ma-Lebona made a shroud and a sheet many years before she died for the day the angel should blow his trumpet to tell her to buy her single ticket for the express journey. As you know she had sores in the chest and almost coughed the roof off I don't know but that woman was made of miracles as sure as your grandfather lies in his grave at Bantule. Ma-Lebona, my grandson, did not want prayer women any more to pray for her because she said they asked God to take her or make her well and Ma-Lebona did not want them to give God a choice as if it would please them either way. You know she and the pastor did not suck from the same breast and I don't know even he was afraid to visit her. She fought with death six months and one day she said to Joel she said Joel I saw death last night and he was ugly so I know more than ever before I don't want to die, and keep those prayer women out Joel, she said again. She said Joel when I'm dead the shroud and the sheet in the box—cover my body with them and my last wish is that you keep the moths out. And then again and again Ma-Lebona did not want to be buried in this new graveyard in Atteridgeville over the hill because it is still full of grass but the one at Bantule where your grandfather lies is good and clean and full of trees. But God is no fool, grandson, so he cured Ma-Lebona and she was up telling us what strong blood she had from her grandfather. Ma-Lebona went to visit some of her people far far away where the sun sets and I don't know but the bridegroom came and took her when her wedding clothes were here. Joel took them to her but the people said where have you seen such a miracle asking us to bury your mother in the things she made and so he returned with the wedding clothes. His mother was buried in a graveyard with thorn trees and no tombstones but only tired ant-eaten wooden crosses and where you smell poverty from far far away. My mother is gone and she was the sixth to be buried in the new Atteridgeville cemetery which Ma-Lebona had disdained. More mothers will come and pass on but the African sage will tell you pain defies comparison. There are many more second avenues with dirty water and flies and children with traces of urine running down the legs and chickens pecking at children's stools. I have been moving up and down Second Avenue since I was born and never dreamt I should ever jump out of the nightmare. Often I wonder if I'm still alive or whether this is not really another way of 'crossing the bar'. . . . The Indian and Chinese shops have turned about and are facing the Indians and the Coloureds looking like deformed creatures of in-breeding.

Twenty

MARRIED

It's customary among both urban and rural Africans today to marry by civil rites and then have the union solemnized in church. The Native Commissioner is the government marriage officer, and a notice of banns is stuck up in his offices while the minister announces them in church on three consecutive Sundays. Most of our people frown on a couple that takes out a special licence from the magistrates' courts to avoid some of the delays and the church ritual most denominations subject a couple to before they can be married. This is where free-lance ministers come in handy. When they have wangled a marriage officer's certificate from the Native Affairs Department they can quickly conduct a marriage service at the usual fee of two pounds, which in any case every denomination charges.

We took the orthodox route. When negotiations had first opened towards the end of 1944, Rebecca's uncles had been tough. They had stood firmly on a bride-price of £60. One of my mother's emissaries had lost his temper during the proceedings and Rebecca's uncles had also lost their tempers. But the day had ended comfortably because two chickens lost their lives to feed the emissaries. Only then, as is the custom, did Rebecca and her mother come out, to serve the guests with food. I couldn't be tolerated on the premises. I had to wait elsewhere until the 'talks' were completely over.

I had felt a groggy sensation when I was told of the £60. Where was I going to rake up such a sum? Arthur Blaxall had given me a job outside office hours, doing secretarial work in preparation for a conference of the Christian Council, of which he was part-time organizer. This way, I had barely collected the £60 in six months and thus, with pride, I had proceeded to claim my bride.

Rebecca detested the whole business transaction as much as I did. But she was, as most women in the same position, helpless. 'You've not come for a calabash that's been thrown on the rubbish heap, or for a broken calabash,' one of the uncles had said. 'Her mother sent her to school,' the other uncle had added, 'and now she's going to lose one leg when the daughter goes.' As if *my* mother's legs were now going to be doubled.

It had been agreed that the bride's mother provide part of the trousseau: the gown and its appendages. We had to buy the frock the bride would change into in the afternoon.

The day came: 29th August 1945. The uncles had bought two oxen for slaughter. There were big crowds of people to feed. A large canvas tent was pitched up for the guests in some part of the yard. Rebecca's mother had asked one of the tenants to vacate a room for special use by Aunt Dora, grandmother, my three uncles, brother and sister, and a few other close relatives. As custom demanded, the hostess had ready a special waitress to cater for the groom's people. Custom also gave the groom's people the prerogative of being fussy and fastidious. Grandmother in particular didn't like the tea, because it wasn't—she would have been surprised if it were—well brewed; she didn't like the flirtatious eyes of their young waitress. Of course, word had long been sent before that she didn't eat beef: mutton had to be procured.

We went to the African Methodist Episcopal Church in Sophiatown for the marriage service. Amid all the jollity, the dancing and *lu-lu-lu-lu-li-li-li* of women in the yard I felt lonely and couldn't shake off the heaviness that was oppressing me because of my mother's absence. I refused to do the folk dance, but Rebecca had to oblige the crowd, and she stepped out into the street with the bridesmaids and groomsmen. I didn't try hard, really, to snap out of my mood.

In the evening we went to the non-European social centre in the city, for a reception. I felt elated during that grand march, and danced through the night, until two o'clock the next morning—

a different man altogether. Rebecca was in buoyant spirits all the time. I even flattered myself that I had made a light-hearted and eloquent speech in reply to the lemonade toast.

The taxi account for the day rocketed to £22. I was supposed to carry the expenses, but I couldn't. My mother-in-law came to the rescue.

In September we went to live in Orlando East, near the high school. The school had procured houses from the municipality for some of its married staff. Ours had just been vacated by municipal tenants. There were only two rooms with an old sunken floor and a sooty hessian ceiling. The school had the floor dug up and new concrete flooring put in. The ceiling was repainted white. During that time we lived on a sandy floor. We paid 17s. 4d. a month for rent.

After about ten months in this house we moved to new houses in Orlando West. We had four biggish rooms to ourselves and boasted the luxury of a pantry, a scullery with a water tap. Over at Orlando East we carried water from a communal tap in the street. The rent in the new house was £2 10s. a month.

From our higher ground Orlando East was a mass of red-roofed blocks, with a population of 100,000. The eastern part had been put up in 1933, twelve miles out of Johannesburg. There was an electrified railway line linking us with the city, and eleven-coach trains, referred to on the time-tables as 'Native trains', carried big loads of people to and from work.

The only beautiful thing about Orlando was the street lights looked at across from our dark west end of the township. And then you saw only the lights and the vague ghostly tanks of the power station on the fringes of the settlement, towering above everything else.

Below us, along the railway line and a small river carrying water from the mines, was Shanty Town. It was then a three-year-old squalid little settlement. Breeze blocks had taken the place of the first tin-and-sack huts that 8,000 squatters had put up after their mighty exodus from the small overcrowded houses of Orlando East. It was an act of protest against the city council for not building more houses for Africans. The council had then built the breeze blocks, cut them up into single rooms, each to hold a family. Corrugated asbestos had been placed on top and stones used to hold it down. Occupants had to transform raw ground into something like a floor.

The squalor and poverty here touched me deeply. I was back in Second Avenue. I tossed and turned in my waking and sleeping hours, and I saw no way out of the mental and spiritual conflicts that were harassing me. In 1947 I decided not to go to church any more. The white press, the white radio, the white Parliament, the white employers, the white Church babbled their platitudes and their lies about 'Christian trusteeship', the 'native emerging from primitive barbarism', 'evangelizing the native', 'white guardianship'. Secular institutions wrenched the pulpit from the Church and cited the Scriptures, and the white man saw himself as an eternal missionary among non-whites. The Church raised an occasional feeble voice of protest. The non-white had for years been taught to love his neighbour—the white man; the non-European preacher, the non-European congregations, had taken refuge in the hope of eternal life. While the white preachers, through sermons broadcast over the radio, told their contented suburban congregations the story of Calvary and individual salvation, white churchgoers felt committed to group attitudes and the maintenance of a mythical white supremacy. Equally, the white preacher felt committed to an ethic he did not dare apply to the necessity of group action against the forces of evil in a setting where such forces have worked themselves up into a savage national attitude said to be based on a Christian sense of justice.

Fellowship? Love? Obedience of the law? Suddenly I did not know what these meant in terms of my place in society, and I revolted against such preachments. How could I adopt an attitude of passive resistance towards the ruling clique and their electorate who a year later were to dedicate themselves to the cause of white supremacy by voting to Parliament a bunch of lawless Voortrekker descendants whose safety lies in the hands of sten-gun-happy police youngsters? How could I even pretend to myself that the

United Party was better, when in 1945 the Smuts government had sent armed troops to quell a riot in a municipal compound near Marabastad, where Africans wanted better living conditions? How could I, when Sturrock of the United Party government had started to rebuild Johannesburg station so that whites and non-whites should enter segregated platforms through segregated entrances? How could anyone unashamedly ask me to do things constitutionally—in obedience to the dictates of an immoral constitution my people did not help formulate?

Something dramatic was taking place inside me. Where I had accepted things as part of a normal programme, my personality revolted. It seemed that there was no escaping from Second Avenue, and that my hate was reconstructing every house in that street. I questioned the necessity of religion. I got stuck and suspended belief and disbelief indefinitely.

Way back in the early 1940's I was writing verse in English which it makes me feel cheap to read today. The idyllic setting of Ezenzeleni was to blame for it. I wrote short stories too. I had never studied the short story form: I was just writing as my feelings dictated. Shortly after coming to Orlando High School in 1945 I sent ten to the African Bookman in Cape Town which had ventured into producing monographs and pamphlets by Africans on political and social subjects. The publisher wrote back to say he wanted to publish five of the stories, adding that he was taking a chance as he had never handled fiction of any kind before. In 1947 the final product was sent to me; a neat little volume with pen drawings for illustrations, under the title *Man Must Live*.

To see myself in print for the first time was an ecstatic experience. The cautious 700 copies were printed in the first edition, almost all of which were disposed of. Not a successful 'first night', but I didn't really care as much as I was proud of the little volume.

The white press was most patronizing in parts, just woolly in others. Said a Johannesburg *Star* critic: 'These stories owe little to the western European tradition. They are more in the Slav tradition. Mr. Mphahlele writes like a Russian . . . These stories are very coolly written. The author stands a little away from this astonishing world he has set out to describe. Yet his stories are full of feeling. . . .'

The *Cape Argus*—Cape Town—blabbered some journalistic who-what-where type of 'criticism', starting off vaguely: '. . . these are phases of African life which no white writer could portray from the same angle.' The *Cape Times* said: '. . . is primarily of interest by virtue of the fact that the author is an African. Both in style and construction, therefore, it is not surprising that his immaturity should be noticeable.' And then, as if to placate me: 'Of all literary forms, the short story is one of the most difficult to master completely.'

The Johannesburg literary magazine, *Trek*, said: 'Instead of blaming fate or God or that popular abstraction, the social system, he—the writer—knows how much of human tragedy is wrought by the ill-will and weakness of people themselves. Thus his stories give us not economic or political theories about human beings, but real people giving and taking, hurting and sacrificing; frail noble mortality, unchanging through the centuries beneath all their apparent alteration.' In contrast to this, was something that appeared in the Cape Town leftist weekly, *Guardian*: 'Unfortunately the author of these stories has had the gods of his fathers exorcized by missionaries. He has forgotten that he is an African. If you changed the names of the characters in his stories, they might be creatures of any race or clime. They believe in ideal love, heavenly justice, patience . . . They have to struggle both with their own inherent weakness of the flesh and spirit and with the selfishness and callousness of others, just like the heroes of Victorian novels. But never once do they complain about the pass laws, the pick-up vans or the insolence of the white man. . . . They are not genuine characters . . . (The writer) should return to his people for inspiration.'

This made me squirm, not because my shortcomings at the time were being spotlighted—I recognized them only too clearly —but because of the half-truths that the critic indulged in: a man who had, as a white man, never needed to carry a pass and go through numerous other humiliations that are the lot of the African.

In the meantime I loved teaching. I loved my extra-mural activities, boxing and dramatics which I introduced in the school. I produced and acted in several one-act plays; parts of Shakespeare; folk tales and scenes from Charles Dickens which I adapted for the stage. I got all the encouragement from a European lady teacher of dramatic art and music in Johannesburg, the third of the small number of European friends I have the pride and pleasure to have. She has always had abundant faith in me, faith I often couldn't sustain.

We even ventured into the Bantu Men's Social Centre in the city, where we enjoyed a multi-racial patronage. Later the whites got scarcer as greater pressure was exerted by those who have taken it upon themselves to direct the lives of whole communities 'according to their own lines', with all the cynical ambiguity the phrase possesses. The powers that be, instead of legislating against the multi-racial audiences those days, were content to wag a finger of cold war at white patrons. It worked. We retreated to our townships 'to develop along our own lines'. We couldn't see the lines and the footprints. They had got so mixed up with other footprints in the course of time, and the winds had been blowing away some, too.

Four years after joining the staff of the high school, I obtained the B.A. degree as an external student of the University of South Africa, majoring in English, Psychology and Native Administration. I also took a degree course in Afrikaans, which I was then teaching as well as English in the matriculation class.

We had one son, Anthony. With my total salary of £42 a month after climbing up gradually from £13 a month, Rebecca and I felt we were rich, compared with what we were during the first years of our married life.

Rebecca herself was teaching for £8 a month. She was sickly, especially after suffering two miscarriages, but she was a divine source of inspiration during those years of hard study. Every year we both scoured the second-hand bookshops for my textbooks to keep down the account on my studies which was near strangling.

I was in my usual rebellious frame of mind when the report of the notorious 'Commission on Bantu Education' was issued; the report according to which the Bantu Education Act was later to be framed. Before I was fully aware of the change that was coming over my outlook on life as a Black man, I found myself in the teachers' movement. I was elected secretary of the provincial body in the winter of 1950.

Already, before the report appeared, I had read a paper at an annual conference of Transvaal African teachers (in South Africa one isn't simply a *teacher*: he is an *African* teacher or a *European* teacher or an *Indian* or *Coloured* teacher). In this paper I criticized the existing so-called 'Code of Syllabuses in Native Primary Schools'. I dismissed the Code as being for a race of slaves; for pupils who were not expected to change as well as be changed by the environment, but to fit themselves into it; for unsettled communities doomed for ever to shift from one place to another, without the necessity to become either a stable peasantry or urban communities. I condemned the textbooks ordered by the Education Department for use in African schools: a history book with several distortions meant to glorify white colonization, frontier wars, the defeat of African tribes, and white rule; Afrikaans grammar books which abound with examples like: *the Kaffir has stolen a knife; that is a lazy Kaffir;* Afrikaans literature that teems with offensive words like *aia*—for non-white women, *outa*—for non-white men, and a literature that teems with non-white characters who are savages or blundering idiots to be despised and laughed at; characters who are inevitably frustrated creatures of city life and decide to return 'home'—to the Reserves.

I taught Afrikaans as a mere duty, and it was a most painful thing for me to feel that, together with my pupils, I was caught up in a situation where a language had been thrust upon us which was the instrument of our oppression and the source of our humiliation. I had to teach Afrikaans verse which was either lyrical vapourings about natural phenomena or fighting talk inspired by the Great Trek, the Transvaal War of Independence and the Anglo-Boer war. Verse that has been and is still being milked dry by Afrikaans literary critics for lack of a new poetic vision or a fresh poetic impulse.

This was the sort of thing that made me even more angry in my attack of the Code of Syllabuses. And yet this Code was considered by Dr. W. Eiselen, who headed the commission, as outmoded on the grounds that it turned out frustrated Black Europeans, cut off from their 'Bantu Culture', and therefore made the 'educated native' a stranger to his people. As the son of a Lutheran missionary, Dr. Eiselen had for many years served as an inspector and then chief inspector of African schools administering the same Code. He suggested a completely new basis for African education. It earned him a job as Secretary for Native Affairs under the Nationalist government.

Even at this stage the president of the Transvaal teachers, Zeph Mothopeng, editor of the teachers' journal, Isaac Matlare, and I, as secretary, travelled during school vacations to the districts to crusade against the recommendations of the Eiselen Report.

We taught in the same high school. Zeph was still the fiery person he was when he paced up and down in his mine boots on St. Peter's stage in our high school days; but he was more disciplined. The then principal of Orlando High, a member of the Dutch Reformed Church—the church of the Nationalist State—warned against offending the Government. He openly campaigned for the Eiselen system during school assemblies, saying at the same time that he would hoist the flag of any government party he was serving under. Africans would for the first time be elevated to sub-inspectorship, he said, a new experience altogether. 'You have children to feed, gentlemen,' he said to us, 'and it won't do for you to be sacked and you're heading for it if you don't stop talking politics.'

The notices of dismissal did come, and we were given no reasons for being discharged. We were not to teach anywhere in the Union. All we had behind us was informed teacher opinion; little else. Teachers had not long before gained a substantial rise in salaries, for what the rise was worth, and they couldn't afford to risk their jobs by openly sympathizing with us. African political leaders were only just waking up to the changes in the educational field and their interest was half-hearted, at best academic. Conditions of employment in the case of African teachers are such that a dismissed person cannot contest the case in court, and the Education Department is not bound to give the reasons for its action.

A number of pupils decided spontaneously to stay out of school in protest against our dismissal. We were arrested on charge of inciting the boycott and consequently public violence. The three of us were locked up for four days at Number 4 Fort Prison and released on bail. During the trial Crown evidence was given by a number of pupils that they had been taken to the local police station and there forced to sign affidavits to incriminate us, on the threat that they would be sent to the reformatory if they refused. We were acquitted. The chairman of the school committee, Mrs. Winifred Hoernle, a European lady who did a good deal of voluntary work among Africans, bitterly attacked us in the white press, calling us 'rebel teachers'. We tried to get our voice heard through the white press, but we failed. We tried to gain an interview with her to discuss the whole matter, but she refused.

I applied for a teaching post in Bechuanaland Protectorate, a British High Commission territory. A reply came that communication had reached them from the provincial department of education that as I had been 'dismissed for subversive activities' I couldn't gain admission into the Bangwato College. That was the first time I learned the 'reason' for my dismissal. Bitterness ate into me like cancer. Mr. Matlare, one of my colleagues, went to teach in Swaziland Protectorate; but after a few months, the Security Branch of the Union's C.I.D. visited the school and a day after he was given summary notice by the school authorities to leave.

Several times I wanted to take a plunge into law. Encouragement from various friends was not wanting. I told myself that I could not succeed as a lawyer; that I was too emotionally strung for a profession that needs a cool head; that I was useless in following or analysing any legal argument. But I know that even if this were not true, I'd not forsake teaching.

For the next year I scoured the city for a job. I entered a factory as an invoice clerk at £4 a week. I was sacked after the first week because I had argued that I possessed the matriculation certificate (I already had the B.A.). 'No, I can't use a matriculant,' the proprietor said. That was a lesson never to parade my learning when looking for a job. I simply presented myself as I was. If I didn't get another job straight away, at least I wasn't offensive. Not that I would have cared an inch. But walking about like that, the keg of heartburn I was, there was no saying what might happen. I was 'Jimmed' and 'boy-ed' and 'John-ed' by whites.

I managed to escape arrest for not carrying the right kind of pass. I was masquerading as a teacher, with the old document on me.

As a teacher, I had to carry a sheet of foolscap paper saying in my capacity I was exempt from the pass laws but not from curfew regulations. Curfew hours applied only in the case of Africans—11 p.m. to 4.30 a.m. the following day. This document was valid only as long as one was an active teacher. What it meant was that I did not need to carry a pass renewable every month, signed every month by an employer, and becoming invalid as soon as the bearer stopped working for a registered employer. Still, the sheet of foolscap paper didn't render one immune from police interception and inquiry. But when I was teaching, I was stopped several times for a pass and locked up in police cells for not having a special pass under the curfew regulations.

When I realized that I couldn't masquerade any more without exposing myself to harsher treatment and the risk of being whisked off to a Bethal prison farm, I decided to go and queue up for a reference book. That was the exit from a semi-privileged class. I first had my photograph taken at the Pass Office after being regimented by a man with a very red face with lines round the neck like a rhino's. It cut inside me like a razor-blade to be regimented this way, and I felt as if there were a liberal leak in a bag of gall somewhere deep inside my stomach. I used to believe that if I had so much sympathy for the utterly illiterate thousands who moved from one job to another to the tune of rubber-stamps and paper-thumbing, I wouldn't feel the humiliation overmuch when I should queue for a pass. I realized I had cheated myself.

The next thing was to present a slip of paper at the first official's desk in a long line. The paper came from the Orlando superintendent, certifying that I was a registered tenant of his location. The clerk then gave me the reference book—the pass—and stuck one photograph on to a page. He insisted on having a Sotho first name from me to enter into the book. I told him I was never called by a Sotho name. He looked angry and disgruntled at once.

I moved on to the next clerk. He produced two cards, filled in the information about me and duplicated it. Another photograph of me was stuck on to one card and filed. Then to the next one. The big man in the influx control machinery, armed with a large rubber-stamp that could send a man packing in twenty-four hours to quit the city. He it was who was supposed to reduce the number of what they called 'redundant natives' in his municipality; to issue a heavily prescribed permit to look for work; to register every employer and his worker or workers so as to control the Black man's movements everywhere and at all times. A rubber-stamp came down on one of the pages of my book, giving me permission to look for work in Johannesburg. When I found employment, my boss would have to sign his name in the book every month and write 'discharged' if and when he should kick me out or I should decide to leave him. But this would only be after another rubber-stamp had come down to give me permission to stay in Johannesburg as long as I worked there. If I later failed to get 'suitable' employment and the big man got tired of renewing my permit to look for work, down would come his stamp sending me to Pretoria, my place of birth, there to go through the same process.

Rebecca was expecting a third baby, and our savings dried up. That Christmas of 1952, the year we were dismissed, went unnoticed. Then I got a job as a lawyer's second messenger. My senior was a glorified messenger who wrote up the books occasionally. As I could type, I often helped the white girl typist. One day I was told not to type in the reception-room any more as it embarrassed the white clients to run straight into a Black man's face as they entered. 'Take the machine into your waiting-room,' the employer said, 'where you make tea.'

I had to go to the Post Office every day. More often than I had bargained for. A white youngster at the counter took great delight in shouting at us on the 'Non-Europeans Only' side to stand in straight queues or else he wouldn't serve us.

'You've got freckles,' he said to me in Afrikaans when I gave him money for stamps.

'And so? It shows more ugly on you whites,' I replied in his language. I was just too tired from running up and down tall buildings to want to be worked up. So I just slipped into neutral gear and coasted down unfeelingly.

'Jesus, you speak Afrikaans bloody well,' he said. 'Where did you learn it?'

'At school'

'I bet you can't write it as well as I can write English.'

'Try?'

'O.K. You write an essay in Afrikaans and I write one in English, and we look at each other's work.'

I agreed, but didn't do it. The next day he gave me his exercise book, although I didn't have mine.

During those months when I ran errands in town I got used to seeing that breed of white men who seem to be children of the same father: liftmen. I found the majority of them physically disabled, a disgruntled tribe, for ever waging a silent war with eternity. A shabby version of St. Peter, holding the clue as to where you shall go if you're black.

Often it was a goods lift they directed me to. And then it lumbered up seventeen to twenty-one stories. Or I went to the one for 'NATIVES' which started from the first floor or from the cool neutral basement. About four lifts served Europeans at His

Majesty's Building (which housed the city's grand theatre, the inside of which I had never seen). Advocates' chambers were upstairs. Each of the liftmen here allowed Africans to mix with the whites if the former ostentatiously held a file or document or pile of letters: in this case it must have been concluded that he was bound for chambers. Otherwise, as happened when I was calling on an acquaintance in the building, one of the liftmen might give me a piercing look and with tight lips say: 'Fox Street!' That's where the goods lift started; the last resort of all messengers, and the only one for all the cleaners and watchmen in the building. A few times I enjoyed the tight-lipped gravity of these old gentlemen and stood in front of any of the lifts which was not going to move soon; just as if I wanted a lift. It struck me that the man was a custodian of something that was always threatening to be a new order, but was blissfully unaware of the seriousness of his mission. He seemed to rely entirely on an instinctive response mechanism, such as his lift operated on. All he seemed conscious of was that he was trying in his own cripple fashion, and with a vigilance becoming a South African white, to keep alive that dying art of catapulting people up and down on lifts; dying, because some of the lifts in town were unattended. I was always apprehensive when I entered a lift that had no attendant and found myself among a group of whites. Some looked at me as if I were an owl that had blundered into daylight. But they did nothing more than look at me.

Once I missed a 'Native' lift and naïvely asked the European liftman to allow me into his. He looked at me with the face of a Red Indian chief—Hollywood version—and said, pointing judiciously, 'There are the stairs.' I looked behind me, and there were well-polished stairs indeed.

The man I worked for was just another South African lawyer. All wrapped up in his money-making business. Looking at his bronze-like features, his cunning eyes, his thin unbroken moustache, I often wondered if he had a family; if he could fondle a child or wife. It just didn't seem likely. He had tons of drive, and he barked at everybody, black or white. The months I spent in his employ reaffirmed my disinclination to study law. I wouldn't know how to turn into such a creature.

'Mr. Michael didn't believe it when I told him you've the B.A. degree,' my senior said one day.

'What?'

'Hm-m.'

'You shouldn't have told him.'

'Nothing wrong, you do have the B.A. after all. And Miss Preston was excited about it all too.'

I didn't like the whole story. I knew things must blow up sooner or later. Miss Preston, the junior typist, was genuinely interested in my achievements, as far as she could do so under the vigilance of the much harder senior typist, Miss Chimes.

The tribe of white laɑy typists in town was another absorbing object of study for me those days. As a messenger I was bound to go through them in every office. They seemed to do little more than let their bodies sway at their compressed dehydrated hips; perch like brittle china on their seats and paint their nails; pick up a mirror and adjust hair that didn't want adjusting and powder their bloodless faces; hold interminable conversations over the telephone and giggle in a sickening high tone that gave me the itch to hold their jaws open to get full-throated laughter out of them.

'Wait, John,' one with a dehydrated bosom would say, 'the boss is still busy in his office.' While I waited I speculated upon the daily run of these people's lives. While we shouted and laughed in our packed and stuffy trains, in our long, long weary bus queues, in the buses, they boarded their clean buses and separate train coaches from their separate platforms, and travelled to their separate suburbs—clean, quiet but either dead or neurotic. And at our end of life Black humanity, though plunged into a separate, overcrowded, violent and dark existence; still vibrant, robust, with no self-imposed repressions. I wondered what manual work those white hands had ever done. Most likely none. There were Black domestic servants at their beck and call. Those red or pink nails, those thin lips that looked like the paper flowers we used to keep on our table in Marabastad.

The typists liked to send their 'office boys' to the shops to buy fish and chips, flowers, sandwiches, or to the dry cleaners. One of them had a passion for dry cleaners, and was in the habit of playing the Sultan's daughter's game on me. I refused the role of a large black dumb eunuch, after a time, and would not run her private errands. Almost in the same week, a girl in another office said to me: 'You must come again this afternoon, boy.'

'What makes you think I'm a boy and not a girl?' I replied aggressively.

'Now don't you be rude to me!' she said.

'I seem to have come to the right school for manners I see.'

'Now you leave before I call the police.'

I recited to her the number every white man and woman is supposed to know off by heart for dialling the police Flying Squad in cases of burglary and so on.

She did nothing of the sort, and I left, feeling pleased with myself. I should have known it would happen. Twice I had flung back an insult like that, more crudely, when I worked at Ezenzeleni Blind Institute. The aggrieved persons had rung up Mr. Blaxall to complain. All Mr. Blaxall had done was to call me and find out the facts. The matter had ended there. Not so with my lawyer. Not so with the disgruntled typist. I got the sack, and lost a handsome £21 in monthly salary, after working only three months.

My European friends came to the rescue often just when we were on the verge of starving. But I was too proud to ask for more. Zeph Mothopeng, my ex-colleague, had almost similar experiences. No liberal charitable agency would employ us either. 'We receive a government subsidy,' they said, 'and we can't risk it by taking you.'

I had been paying compulsory premiums to the unemployment insurance fund when I was teaching. So there was about £60 for me to draw in fortnightly instalments of five guineas at a time. The offices were on the municipal Pass and Influx Control premises. I reported every week as the law demanded. Here I joined one of the many queues of Black men, each holding a bunch of papers he understood little or nothing about, but which directed their lives hither and thither. They moved from one office to another of the many, to have their papers rubber-stamped by white officials. Papers telling their bearers where they may work or stay and where not; papers telling others that they must go back to the Reserves if they won't accept farm labour under white employers; the same to men from outside the Union, called in official parlance 'foreign natives'. And while I waited, prospective white employers came and announced the jobs they were offering: 'kitchen boy, £4 a month'; 'truck driver, £3 a week'; 'garden boy, 6s. a day for two days in the week'; 'builders (not technically bricklayers), £3 a week'. They shouted, and men milled about, disdaining this job and accepting that, pretending there was much choice. They were like livestock at a fair. African constables shouted for them to go this way and that; like most other African civil servants who overact in asserting their authority, outdoing the master at his work. Most of these men and youths with papers in their hands spent several days at the Pass Office trying to get over one paper hurdle and another, shuffling for ever within the stark, sooty, cold and cheerless walls of the buildings. An African came to me and said he could sell me a pass if I paid him £10 deposit and £5 when I got it. Weeds of corruption grew rank in this dismal jungle of controls. A number of European and African Pass Office clerks and messengers were appearing in the courts on counts of corruption involving the selling of passes for fees mounting up to £20 a pass. Even if I did need a pass desperately I could ill afford to pay £15.

Outside the premises, Indian and Syrian cheapjacks and fat greasy African women sold trinkets and food to these Pass Office pilgrims.

I landed a part-time job as a typist in a Jewish millinery shop which sold articles of clothing to African domestic workers in the suburbs. I earned £10 a month. Rebecca, always the expert housewife as well as a superb cook, got us through our difficulties admirably. Besides, she is a thorough-going optimist; she can steam ahead with long-term schemes without much worry about mishaps.

Twenty-One

CHURCH SHILLINGS

One evening Father Wardle, C.R., then in charge of Holy Cross Anglican Church in Orlando, visited me.

'It's about your church shillings,' Father Wardle said, after we nibbled at topics of general conversation. 'Between you and your wife there is £2 7s. owing. I know things are difficult for you these days, but I just thought I should remind you. Another thing is your attendance at church. Do you find it difficult to reconcile your religion with your politics?'

'Extremely so,' I said.

'Have you tried praying about it?'

'Yes. I've given up trying to pray—formally I mean. I just think and think and think.'

'It's hard for everybody.'

'Not for the white man.' He dropped his head and toyed with the crucifix suspended on his belt, and the pathos on his face annoyed me a little.

Father Wardle couldn't have come at a worse moment about these things. About the same week a young man I used to teach at the high school had come to seek advice about a case he had against the African police at the local station. They had met him in the township and demanded his pass. When he produced it they said it was not genuine, and arrested him. At the station they had caught hold of him and stretched him on a bench while a white constable beat him with a leather belt on bare buttocks. They had then released him. He showed me the weals and I took him to a medical doctor for a certificate. We had laid a charge at the same police station, and the young man had identified the policeman who beat him.

Every time the case came on, it was reported that the constable couldn't attend. I wrote to the District Commandant of Police about this and we had to give it up eventually.

The young man's case recalled to mind, then, that of Rebecca who had been assaulted six months before by a white ticket examiner in a train. There was an argument about a ticket, and the white man had used abusive language and pulled her out of the train at a station with such force that Rebecca had sprained her ankle. She had laid a charge but the man had never appeared in court. Every time he was reported ill. She had then paid a lawyer £15 to take up a civil case against the man. A year after the incident the man, still in the railways, was forced to attend as it was a civil case. He was found guilty and ordered to pay Rebecca £10 damages! That was much later, after our interview with Father Wardle. Rebecca had just had another postponement of the case when the young man came. Yes, Father Wardle couldn't have come at a worse moment.

'Just now, I don't think it's fair for anybody to tell me to expect a change of heart among a bunch of madmen who are determined not to cede an inch, or to listen to reason. It is unfair to ask me to subsist on mission school sermons about Christian conduct and passive resistance in circumstances where it is considered a crime to be decent; where a policeman will run me out of my house at the point of a sten gun when I try to withhold my labour. For years I have been told by white and Black preachers to love my neighbour; love him when there's a bunch of whites who reckon they are Israelites come out of Egypt in obedience to God's order to come and civilize heathens; a bunch of whites who feed on the symbolism of God's race venturing into the desert among the ungodly. For years now I have been thinking it was all right for me to feel spiritually strong after a church service. And now I find it is not the kind of strength that answers the demand of suffering humanity around me. It doesn't even seem to answer the longings of my own heart.'

The priest sat and listened. Again the pathos on his face annoyed me because I didn't know whether it reflected failure to understand the forces that were tearing inside me, or a feeling of pity.

'What *are* the longings of your heart?'

'What every man longs for which he begins to feel sharply when you whites make him feel insufficient.'

'You talk as if I represented the institution of white oppression,' he said.

'That's a tragedy the most decent of us are caught up in whether they like it or not.' I felt a devilish sort of pride in saying so, because that was one of the many times I have wished I could hate all whites: it would be so much simpler and less painful.

'You mustn't misjudge the missionaries, though, after all you were educated in mission schools and your children are in an Anglican nursery school. No government ever thought of building schools for you before the missionary came here, still less, nursery schools.'

'The age-old argument. Still you must admit that before Father Trevor Huddleston came on the scene—and that's only 1943—missionaries had let politics alone and consequently the forces of evil have had a start of about 300 years. During which time missionaries have abetted, connived at or stood aloof from, the white man's total disregard of justice and other human values. Even so, Trevor Huddleston was a lone fighter. The rest of the church in South Africa didn't speak his language.'

'Can I help you in this terrible conflict?'

'No one can help me. I intend to resolve it myself. There are more urgent matters than that. Like the buzzing and groaning and shrieking noises you hear in Shanty Town down there. A resolution of my personal conflicts could never alleviate the miseries of Shanty Town.'

I felt hollow, flat and I feared perhaps in my emotional outburst I had failed to make my point. Maybe I didn't really have a definite point. I told myself that I needed time to think, but really, I couldn't think. And my overcharged emotional response mechanism was my enemy. It has often been. All I knew was that my outlook on the Church had decidedly changed.

A few weeks later Father Wardle refused to baptize our third-born. Rebecca insisted on having him baptized. Little as I cared, I had decided not to stand in her way. But I knew that she was following a custom, and not a conviction, because we shared our disillusionment. From my own standpoint, I didn't feel competent to challenge her to it. Father Wardle's reasons for refusal were that if I didn't believe in the Church any more, and I owed money to the Church I had no right to its sacraments. But then I hadn't claimed any. Still, after a conscientious church councillor had urged him to change his mind, I had to be in our church that afternoon. I didn't even try to be mentally present. The service floated before me like the traffic in front of my house.

After that service I realized all the more how I hated formalism, especially when it contained an element of mysticism; how I detested formal allegiance to groups other than those closely connected with the arts and with the struggle to attain freedom. It had to be something I could *experience* within my then contracting pattern of sensory, emotional and mental responses. And I had outgrown the aesthetic experience of church worship.

I had my firm loyalties. I was steering a Syndicate of Artists, which was promoting classical concerts and under the aegis of which I was producing and acting in plays. Most of our players were those who had started off with me at the high school and were teachers, clerks, nurses, messengers, factory workers, but there was the perennial problem of insecurity, and we continually lost members who had to go and live outside Orlando. There was also the problem of transport and we couldn't walk the streets of Orlando at night for fear of assaults and killings. We had to do our rehearsals on Sunday afternoons. Our audiences loved scenes from Shakespeare, my adaptations of Dickens and folk-tales. A folk-tale that captivated the people more than any other was one I had selected from a collection of Venda tales—from the northern Transvaal—which is very similar to Keats's *Isabella* in plot. I improvised a pantomime scene where the maiden plants a tree in an earthen pot and waters it with her tears, while there is African folk music in the background. We always used tree branches for our stage scenery.

Church Shillings

One Sunday afternoon we took a mixed programme to Germiston, fifteen miles from Johannesburg. We had been invited by a cultural group to perform in the location, one of the slummiest in the whole country. We presented scenes from Shakespeare's *Julius Caesar*; Khabi Mngoma sang a recitative and aria from the *Messiah*; his wife, Grace, contralto, also sang a recitative and aria from the *Messiah* and *My Task*; Milton Oersen the Coloured concert pianist played a sonata and two shorter things by Scarlatti.

Outside the little location hall, as we waited for patrons to go in, a European man came to have a chat, evidently with the motive of making himself known. He was a mine compound manager. I wondered whether we were or he was in the right place. Although a compound manager looks after the African mine workers and clerical staff, one thinks of the brood of managers only in terms of the tribal dances they organize in the mines for American tourists: males in grey palm beach suits looking exasperatingly smug, pockets and seams and cheeks and hairy arms all bulging with 'foreign aid'; beside them, cigarette-smoking women with painted talons, looking excited about nothing in particular. What would a compound manager be doing at such a concert—or at any other? He started in Fanakalo, a stupid mixture of all the Bantu languages with English and Afrikaans, which originated in the mines, where white officers and workers don't particularly like their instructions to be misunderstood by their 'boys'.

'Mina bukile lo programme'—I've been looking at the programme—he said, waving the sheet at Khabi.

'Yini wena kumbula?'—what do you think of it—Khabi said, obviously trying very hard to raise himself to the level of this distinguished patron. I think Khabi was careful not to allow his good English to foil his attempts.

'Yena moshle stellek lo Handel'—Handel is very good.

'Wena aikona funa Scarlatti?'—You don't like Scarlatti?

'Oh, yes, mina thanda lo Scarlatti. Uphi yena cula Scarlatti?'—Oh yes, I love Scarlatti. Who's going to sing him?

Khabi pointed at Oersen, who looked as much like a singer as

Yehudi Menuhin resembles a Cape coon. The pianist looked at Khabi and then at the manager with a poker face.

'Mina jabula kakhulu very much'—I'm very, very happy. Then he proceeded to tell us how some of his 'boys' simply doted on Harry James and Tex Ritter and clamoured for more films showing the trombonist and the cow-punching guitarist.

The performance came off beautifully. After the programme our distinguished patron came up to us backstage.

'That was a wonderful performance,' he said in English, shooting out his paw to confirm his words.

'Tina zamile,' Khabi took up the Fanakalo thread. 'Sibongile stellek, yena moshle stellek lo Scarlatti.'—Well, we've tried. Thank you very much, Scarlatti's very good. A burst of laughter sent the manager's blood up to his ears, and he left the room quickly, to return to his 'boys'.

The funds of the Syndicate were running low as we were staging a number of charity concerts, like those we held in aid of the African School Feeding Scheme, then under the chairmanship of Father Huddleston. The Government had withdrawn its school feeding scheme for Africans and retained it for European children. We turned to more profit-making concerts, but white patrons were too scared to attend because multi-racial audiences were now the focus of the Nationalist Government's wrath. We never lost our aim, which was chiefly to bring serious music and the arts to the doorstep of our people, who were not allowed to go to white theatres or concert halls. We sponsored the exhibitions of two African painters and at our invitation Isobel Baillie, the British singer, and Victor Mcunu, the African tenor, came to perform to multi-racial audiences.

The last half of 1953 I worked for Arthur Blaxall as shorthand-typist. He had retired from active blind welfare work, and was secretary of the Christian Council of South Africa. I was paid £20 per month, and he added £8 from his own pocket.

In December I began to kick my heels again. I was dying to be back in the classroom more than ever before. The yearning was choking me and I felt my nerves were giving in. An excruciating sense of inadequacy assailed me. I reflected that it wasn't so much the loss of a higher income that was telling on me, crippling though that was, as the feeling that my professional integrity had been questioned, and there was no way of my vindicating myself.

I took a blind shot at a post in a Basutoland Protectorate high school. In January I was called by the school to join its staff as English and geography master. For the second time in my life I left the employ of Arthur for a teaching job. That January my friend Zeph and I went down to Maseru, leaving our families behind. He had been there six months ahead of me. A report about our 'subversive activities' had already reached the administration in the Protectorate, but nothing came of it.

I began studying for the B.A. honours degree in English. The project occupied most of my time outside school, so that the first six months didn't drag. I did the degree for the sheer love of studying English. I loved particularly the papers on practical criticism, poetics, Shakespeare and Victorian literature. Gerard Manley Hopkins kept me company in my lonely moments and when I climbed the mountain nearby, from which to view the majesty, the grandeur that is Moshoeshoe's country.

It was no economic gain to be in Basutoland. Teachers are paid poorly there and progress is very slow, which are the reasons why most of the country's progressive teachers are in the Union. My salary was £23, compared with the Union's £43 and Arthur's £28. I did more thinking in Basutoland than I had ever done before. I had toyed with the idea of making it my home. But life was stagnant; people apathetic; the civil servants looked miserably bogged down. People had no cultural interests, and I have never been a crusader. I have tons of energy for work when I don't have to organize and direct the activities of adults. And then I had become thoroughly urbanized and couldn't feel happy in such a country.

Interlude

I went to Basutoland in search of something. What it was I didn't know. But it was there, where it wasn't, inside me. Perhaps it was hate, maybe love, or both; or sordidness; maybe it was beauty. As I say, I didn't know. Once I had landed on the soil of Moshoeshoe's country, the quest seemed never to come to an end. I'm not even sure it has, yet. I stood one night a few yards away from the foot of a hill. You find solid, palpable darkness in Basutoland. I tried to rip the dark with the razor edge of my desire; but I found nothing to ease the heaviness of my soul. I scoured the sky with my eyes; in my fancy I raked the stars together, leaving a sieve in the velvet sky. Then I collected them and splashed the sky with them. Some of the stars were pulverized in transit and chalked the blue with a milky way. You know, it reminded me of the powder of an exhausted moth-killer. Still, I couldn't find it. Mars's yellow lustre told me nothing. How could it?—an inquisitive visitor come to see me wriggle and squirm, crawl and cringe, to hear me curse and grouse and commune with the infinite, and then to turn and go, cold and unmoved. The autumn trees might tell me something, I thought. Brown and yellow leaves fluttered in the air, and landed with arrogant smugness on the ground. The trees themselves stood about like debauched men.

I followed the tacking of long-tailed *monope* till he perched upon a tree with an aristocratic bow; *tsemedi*, the hangbird, gave a spiteful screech to mock a dove's cooing; a swarm of birds moved as if on the crest of a changing wave; the reconnoitring hawk glided with wings in full span, poised for a deadly dive.

I went to the top of a high mountain. There I felt the touch of the Ultimate, but only for a fleeting dizzy moment. Below were fields laid waste by rushing water: fingers and fingers of furrows with photographic unreality. Grey earth cried out in vain to the skies; as grey and fruitless as the cough of old men who cry for the migrant sons in mine pits of far-away lands, where their lungs began to rot.

For one brief moment of rich promise I thought the secret was in the conical hat and the blanket of a Mosuto standing placidly on the edge of a summit at sunrise. But perhaps he also was dawn's pilgrim.

You get a feeling of static life in Moshoeshoe's country: you see a man on a stationary horse or pony; the static grandeur of the mountains seeming to approach and recede at the same time, at once defiant and reassuring; structures of *maseru* stone that is quarried in Maseru and which lends an air of permanence; the gorges left by the claws of Time; villages on the flat mountain-tops in spite of the scanty food crops that grow there; fat lazy sheep that seem to have been on a grass patch since the beginning of time; the Bushmen rock painting; Thaba Bosiu, which still breathes the spirit of Móshoeshoe's majesty, but as mute as the Sphinx, a legend that has sought immortality in stone and earth. Every scene is complacently static, often annoyingly so. Even the faces of Basuto were static. Yet their classical outer appearance conceals the romantic rage of a roaring flood.

My longing search continued. Mind and heart stood still. It tormented me to feel so insufficient, and not to know the why and wherefore. At times thought and feeling would gush forth in torrents so that many things became jumbled symbols of my hope and yearning: the purple-pink sunsets; the wasting bleached earth; the rock hanging precariously on the cheek of a hill; the muddy grey waters of the Caledon; the eternal streak of cloud lying stretched out like one of heaven's drunken sots. But alas, my dreams had long since taken flight and now hung dry in shining cobwebs to which my fermenting furies clung crucified. . . .

Then an old man visited me. Arthur. We talked the night away, confiding in each other, learning from each other.

Dawn came and announced victory. The quest had come to an end, if the mere knowing of it seems to be the end.

I knew then what I had been looking for: a fatally beautiful lady called bitterness. I knew I had wanted to love her, caress her, kiss her; but not, in Swinburnian fashion, to be bitten to death by her. Only if I chased after and loved her could I strangle her. I could hang her up to dry and show her up to the mockery of the elements.

She's in my arms now. I do not kiss her any more: the blue fire of our kisses has turned white; she has bitten my lips, I have sucked hers dry that not so long ago looked like a full-blown sail in a coquettishly sensuous pout. I've tamed her. She's the mistress of my dull useless moments; so I can stamp my foot on the ground to have her once proud head chopped off—the head that once launched a million corpuscles in my blood which chafed against the roots of my hair. But I may not just decide. Depends on the other man. Tell it him.

Twenty-Two

DRUM

I did not return to the Protectorate in August. Instead, I accepted a request from my former high school, St. Peter's, to teach Afrikaans and Mathematics. But I couldn't be recognized by the Government, and so I was paid from school funds—£18 a month.

Rebecca had all but broken down when I was in Basutoland; from excessive worry about her budget. She was terribly thin.

At the end of the year, Father Trevor Huddleston, then superintendent of St. Peter's, offered to double my salary during the following year. But that was to be the last year in the life of the school, because it was 'discovered' by the Minister of the Interior that it was in an area for whites. I had to move. Of course, the Community of the Resurrection had planned to carry on as a private school, rather than lease the premises to the State to carry out its Bantu Education under the new Act based on the Eiselen Commission's Report. It meant that after 1956 I should be in the streets again. So I had to accept a £25 job as journalist and literary editor of *Drum* monthly magazine in Johannesburg, then edited by Anthony Sampson.

In November I had written the honours examination. I almost gave up in the middle of the examinations, feeling mentally fatigued. But by sheer luck I held on, and I passed.

I had no illusions at all about my inability to become a journalist. My whole outlook resisted journalism: my attitude towards the white press; towards the double stream of newspaper policy in South Africa where there is a press for whites and a press for non-whites; towards *Drum's* arbitrary standard of what the urban African wants to read: sex, crime and love stories; its use of

Sophiatown as the yardstick of what the South African non-white should read. It was to the credit of Anthony Sampson and even more of that daring reporter, the late Henry Nxumalo, that *Drum's* annual exposures of social and political evils were the dynamic piece of journalism they deserved to be. I served under Anthony Sampson for three months and under his successor, Sylvester Stein, for the next twenty-seven months.

I tried to be happy in the job that interested me more than reporting—the editing of short stories. Even here I was supposed to let in the 'wet sentimental sexy stories and tough crime stories'. I tried to argue with the proprietor whenever he interviewed me that *Drum* had plunged into a reading world which hadn't developed any definite magazine taste (the non-European readership); that it should produce healthy material in an original style wherever possible and, in a sense, dictate what the public should read, without necessarily being snobbish and intellectual. He told me that it wasn't *Drum's* mission. Even as a sub-editor, I could feel the pressure of 'policy' through the editor. I suspected that he was also chafing against the walls of a cage dropped from above. But I think Sylvester Stein's eagerness, dash, and ability to throw himself into a thing as if it was all that mattered at the time, didn't allow him to be frustrated. Or perhaps I could afford to show frustration where he couldn't.

About seven of my own short stories which I had the conceit to think were not vulgar escapist stuff managed to find their way into the magazine. Most of the time I felt like a bull without a china shop.

It was later in 1955 that I joined the African National Congress (ANC). I had for some years been torn between it and the All-African Convention (AAC). The verbal war that had been going on between them since 1935 was still raging at the time in these terms:

AAC: Your Jabavu and Matthews and the rest of them sold out to Hertzog and accepted that dummy parliament, the Native Representative Council.

ANC: You broke away from the alliance to start with.

AAC: How could we stay in it when you refused to boycott dummy institutions and toy telephones?

ANC: Trouble is you theorize too much and you're out of touch with the masses. When are you ever going to act?

AAC: We're not adventurists and careerists like you.

ANC: Cowards!

AAC: You've got to educate the masses politically first.

ANC: Who's to say when they'll be educated?

AAC: When they've ceased to be duped by you into electing white reactionaries into Parliament and pushing your own provincial presidents into dummy advisory boards—cheating the people into thinking they've something real.

ANC: We must capture the platform wherever we can. Do you expect us to leave the stooges to go in?

AAC: If the stooges know they'll be isolated and labelled Quislings they'll have no one to represent.

ANC: Let's not be dogmatic. If the people want leadership, let's give it them on any platform which we can seize without compromising ourselves. Such a platform has nuisance value. That's how Matthews and the lot brought the Representative Council to a dead stop and got themselves disbanded by the Government.

AAC: Communist infiltration tactics again. It doesn't stop there. Now it's the white Liberals you're flirting with and they're the ones telling you to use democratic and constitutional methods of struggle. Soon you'll be co-operating with the United Party.

ANC: You're being cynical. When we do co-operate we choose wisely, and then it's in matters of common interests and our allies don't run our affairs—what's wrong with that?

AAC: That's unprincipled co-operation—like your weak-kneed multi-racial Planning Council which dragged the masses into a futile Defiance Campaign.

ANC: First you say we're racialists and tribalists because of our earlier slogan of African nationalism. Now that we work together with Indian, Coloured and European democratic organizations, we're unprincipled.

AAC: Why not unity, like our Unity Movement?

ANC: We shall not put it off when the day is ripe for it.

AAC: But you still have the three minority organizations. You could join the Unity Movement as a federal body, like us. And then the question of minorities falls away.

ANC: Why don't you join our Congress of the People?

AAC: What happens when the Indian organization does the exact opposite of what ANC may decide—where's the Congress of the People then? Unprincipled again!

ANC: You're afraid of action, that's all.

AAC: Rather that than throw the people into a field to be fodder for police guns before you've organized sufficiently.

And so on the interminable wrangling went on. The facts in the arguments were straight, and their principles overlapped more than either side was prepared to admit, and they were content to shelter behind half-truths. I had for ten years attended meetings and been in discussion groups on both sides and now I considered that I had bounced enough, mentally, between the two walls; that in any case I was committed.

I accepted fully the boycott of statutory political institutions which had been thrown in our midst. At the same time, I couldn't find a home in the intellectual exercise the AAC indulged in at their meetings, and their total contempt for that something among the masses which yearns for protest marches and rallies. I think also that I accepted some of the AAC's politics as a defence against the possibility of feeling exclusively African. Instinctively I treasured the thought that I bore not real bitterness against Indians and Coloureds. I even thought at one time that it was very urgent that we should come to such a closely knit non-white group that the question of minorities wouldn't arise. But I remembered that the ANC had been founded because the Africans felt they were being discriminated against as a national group. So I learned to be content with the fact that the ANC had shaken off its chauvinism of the 1940's, and with the present close co-operation between the Indian Congress, the Coloured People's Organization and the white Congress of Democrats.

Whenever opportunity presented itself I preached unity between ANC and AAC. For lack of a better epigram, I said the AAC could do with more emotionalism and an enterprising spirit; the ANC, with more absolutes and the AAC with fewer. At present the ANC initiates campaigns for the AAC to intellectualize upon.

There are things it is not easy to say when one is caught up in a mighty sweep of events that cannot wait too long for concerted political action such as it behoves a multi-racial combine—like that of the Congresses—to take. Away from the clamour of public meetings I had discussions with Indian and Coloured associates and friends. I let them know how worried I was by the 'group area' politics of the Indians and Coloureds. How long, I asked, was the Indian merchant class going to dole out money to support their Congress only when a particular law was being resisted which threatened Indian business? Why had not the Indians ever helped Africans in their fight against, say, the Pass Laws, and only come in when Indian trade was being strangled by group area legislation? Did the Indian value parliamentary and municipal representation or did he just want to be financially safe?

Give the merchant class a chance, my friends said. 'As soon as they realize that without political power economic strength can only be temporary, they'll wake up.'

A coloured friend told me that his organization was little more than a name. He admitted that the only Coloured people who thought seriously about politics were intellectuals in the 'wrong camp'—the Unity Movement. The average Coloured, he also admitted, was more concerned with 'keeping Coloured'—not to be reclassified 'native', be made to carry the pass and to be paid lower wages. 'Defensive politics' was his label.

In the year that I joined ANC, the Bantu Education Act arrived in the African primary school. About the same time Sophiatown, one of the only three freehold townships in Johannesburg for Africans, was being removed, because it was in a 'white area'. I reported these events for *Drum*. On both occasions, the African National Congress was caught with its pants down. The leadership had never really interested itself in educational and cultural matters as an important flank to its activities. All its time had been taken up in organizational work around purely political ideology. Resistance to these two measures failed. Haphazardly the ANC tried to jolt the morale of the masses by means of slogans. In the case of Sophiatown, the movement did not reckon with the big tenant population which swarmed the backyards of the township and which would be only too happy to pay about £4 a month for three rooms in Meadowlands, however badly constructed and whatever municipal controls would be waiting for them. In Sophiatown they paid at least £2 for a room.

On the boycott of schools and Bantu Education the leadership were terribly divided and confused. The boycotters did not reckon with the vicious circle that makes it imperative for working parents to leave their children in the care of a school during the day, and that several months are needed to prepare the minds of parents about what Bantu Education means in the classroom, as a tool of oppression.

The churches were no less divided on the issue of the Bantu Education Act. They were being ordered to hand over their school buildings to the Government because the latter couldn't continue to subsidize them for 'teaching the Black man that he can be equal to a white man'. The Johannesburg Anglican Diocese did the painful and therefore courageous thing: it closed down its buildings and refused to have them used for an inferior system of education. Some denominations merely acquiesced to the Government's order without the twitch of a hair. Others again even tried to justify Bantu Education. Dr. J. B. Webb of the Methodist Church told overseas audiences that the new syllabuses were not really bad. The Roman Catholics decided to run private schools, but Dr. Verwoerd, then the Minister of Native Affairs, told them that eventually his department would take them over. At the time of writing, Anglican buildings in Johannesburg are still empty and forsaken.

In spite of a statement by the Institute of Race Relations to the effect that the new syllabuses were not inferior to the old Code the pattern was set: both teacher and pupil were being committed to the *status quo*, as the following items will show:

Subject: Citizenship and Good Conduct (a Verwoerd Patent).

1. Why we need the services of
   (a) the headman, the chief, the policeman, the agricultural officer (overseer: white, if you please).
   (b) the location superintendent (white, if you please).
   How we can assist these officials and professional men in their work.
2. Local government: various Bantu authorities in urban and rural areas (a Verwoerd patent).
3. Instruction and guidance in connection with
   (a) the Personal Reference Book (this is the Pass. The gentle epithet *personal* is meant to allay the Black man's fears).
   (b) the Labour Bureaux and how they work.
   (And *how*! The term should be Labour Auction Mart.)
   (c) control measures in urban areas—control of the movement into and out of urban areas; reasons for this.

Subject: Environment Study (a Verwoerd patent).

The different types of work done by people in the area surrounding the school and the *contributions they make to the happiness and progress of the community* (my italics):
   (a) the chief and his councillors;
   (b) the farmer (white, if you please, with a keen nose for the smell of cheap labour);
   (c) the shopkeeper (white, if it is in the rural areas);
   (d) the officers of the Native Trust (white).

Under the syllabus for 'History and Social Life' is seen a fat finger wagging in the form of:

Remarks: Only the most important facts connected with the settlement of Europeans at the Cape should be imparted to the pupils.

While on *Drum* I also covered the big bus boycott that rocked the country and scared big financial houses almost out of their wits. Bus fares had been raised in Johannesburg and Pretoria by a penny, with the Government's consent. When 'sympathy boycotts' sprang up in other parts of the country and the people said, 'when we are tired of walking we sit down at home', the whites got really frightened. The white press at first became sanctimonious about the Black man's economic plight which the boycott 'had brought to light'. But later, the white press became openly hostile to the boycotters.

Another big event I reported on was the march of 20,000 African women to the Union Buildings in Pretoria, where they handed in signed protests against the Government measure to force women to carry passes. Prime Minister Strijdom was not in and the documents were left in his office. The leader of the women, Lilian Ngoyi, held them spellbound during twenty minutes' silence, while they stood in front of the buildings with their thumbs up. The irony couldn't escape me of the Black Sash women (Europeans only) standing their usual shifts at the entrances in order to move government men to restore the character of the Constitution as at 1910; and there, in the pit just below the Black Sash, thousands of dark voices were telling government men to tear to pieces the 1910 document and reconcile themselves to multi-racial rule.

Always I felt too deeply to be objective in my reporting and I was subjected to rigorous editorial censoring. That did not pain me so much as the necessity to be in *Drum* when I did not really want to be a journalist. I wanted to teach and I wanted to be a writer. During those thirty months, I had to live two lives. A life of sub-editing and reporting and fiction editing during the day, and a life of study and creative writing in the night. Try hard as I might, I couldn't find a comfortable meeting point between the two. My prose was suffering under severe journalistic demands and I was fighting to keep my head steady above it all. I felt like a slow-footed heavyweight, wanting to be sure of every punch, in a ring which required a disposition to duck and weave and gamble and love the game or quit.

In 1956 I began research for a thesis which I was going to present for the M.A. degree in the University of South Africa. My subject was *The Non-European Character in South African English Fiction*. The study of Afrikaans literature which has created a stock non-white character led me to inquire into the 'enigma' as it emerged in English fiction. I made a quick survey of English literature inside Africa and outside, where the non-white character is portrayed: Conrad, E. M. Forster, William Faulkner, Kipling, Mulk Raj Anand, Pearl Buck, William Plomer, George Orwell, Harriet Beecher Stowe, Carl van Vechten, Countee Cullen, Langston Hughes, Richard Wright, Claude McKay, Roger Mais, George Lamming, John Steinbeck and David Karp. Then I dealt with the early emergence of the non-white character in South African literature from Thomas Pringle to Rider Haggard; a body of literature where the non-white character appears either as a barbarian on the battlefield or as a noble savage.

Next, I studied four South African novelists of the first rank: Olive Schreiner, Sarah Gertrude Millin, William Plomer, and Alan Paton. Then followed six lesser novelists—lesser only in the sense that their non-white characters do not loom so large and their works have a restricted intellectual and emotional appeal. These were Laurens van der Post, Grenfell Williams and Henry John May, Oliver Walker, Peter Abrahams, Harry Bloom, and Nadine Gordimer.

When I read Peter Abrahams's books I began to understand what it must have meant to him to want to justify himself. He has worked this passion into a dominating symbolism through the characters in his novels—this tragic longing for socially forbidden things. I don't think, as I have often been tempted to think in moments of extreme bitterness, that his *Vision Splendid* has been a mere panting after white patronage. For although a number of factors limit the range of his writings, I have a real admiration for what he has achieved in the literary sphere.

I used E. M. Forster, Joseph Conrad and William Faulkner as my standards for faithful portrayal of non-white character, untrammelled by some such political message or preachments as bedevil South African fiction. The main weakness in South African writers is that they are hyper-conscious of the race problem in their country. They are so obsessed with the subject of race and colour that when they set about writing creatively they imagine that the plot they are going to devise, the characters they are going to create and the setting they are going to exploit, must subserve an important message or important discovery they think they have made in race relations. I admire William Plomer's and Laurens van der Post's poetic sense of irony which, for me, makes the theme of *Turbott Wolfe* more meaningful than Paton's sermon.

And yet, when William Plomer wrote *Turbott Wolfe*, he was writing as a white man who had discovered a new continent with a distinct type of violence, a people with a beautiful culture that was resisting a domineering white culture, and the race attitudes and relations peculiar to such a set-up. When he writes his *Paper Houses* much later, he is more experienced and race contacts no longer arouse in him a romantic revolt or admiration and desire to suggest a solution. He simply writes about human beings and human problems as seen against a class structure which is to be found anywhere outside Japan. For this reason the stories are more important than his novel for their characterization of non-whites. What conflict or reconciliation there is between the Orient and the West is lived by his characters and not a sermonizing outside characterization as in his novel.

I place Olive Schreiner in a class by herself, although, like Plomer, she identifies the non-white character with the setting, of which it is an organic part. Love the one, then you love the other; violate the one, then you violate the other. Plomer chooses to call the reaction of the setting the 'violence of Africa'.

I quote from my thesis:

'Non-whites live in locations, or in the Reserves, or work for whites in towns and on farms, where they are either labour tenants or squatters. There can hardly be a healthy common culture in conditions that isolate whole communities and make social and economic intercourse difficult or impossible. And the problem of a national culture is *per se* the problem of a national literature. It must remain sectional and sterile as long as such conditions prevail.'

At the end of 1956 I submitted my thesis. I was awarded the degree with distinction. It was the first time the Department of English of the University of South Africa awarded a distinction for a senior degree. The University caters for European and non-European external students equally.

Two women stood uppermost in my mind at graduation in the winter of 1957: my late mother—how I wished she were alive—and Rebecca—it was also a day of triumph for her.

There we were, a little over sixty graduands in all, including two Indians, congregated in the small church of Kilnerton Institution, the African boarding school just outside Pretoria, where Rebone had trained as a teacher twenty years before. The graduands were people who were in regular employment and had done their degrees by private study. Exactly two years before, I had come to the same hall to graduate in B.A. honours English. The European graduation ceremony had been held earlier in Pretoria city. Although the University of South Africa had the same tuition by correspondence, the same syllabuses and conducted the same examinations for both its European and non-European students, apartheid forbade a joint ceremony. The principal of the University and the whole academic staff—all Europeans—sat in front of us, looking terribly South African and medieval all at once. Jenny Stein, wife of Sylvester Stein, Arthur and Mrs. Blaxall, who had been invited by us, sat among the audience. Jenny refused to join a small number of whites occupying two benches in the front.

Mr. Kgoare, M.A., M.Ed., a sub-inspector of Bantu Education in the Orange Free State Province, gave the graduation speech. He praised the white people for the education they were giving us; he praised the Education Department for putting up schools for the 'Bantu' in his province which were 'second to none in the country'; he praised the white farmers in his province for building schools on their farms for their workers' children; he excused the Free State whites for their hard-hearted attitude towards Indians, even although the province allowed in no more than the four Indians already resident there. Mr. Kgoare received no applause from the African audience whatever. Only the whites of the University gave him a hand-clap.

When my turn came I seemed to be moving on an escalator to the Chancellor's seat. I had the loudest and longest ovation of the afternoon from the packed hall.

When the graduates and guests and staff had tea later, the whites again, excepting my invitees, segregated themselves. They drank out of complete tea sets while we had an assortment of oddly-matched cups and saucers.

The next day an Afrikaans morning paper in Johannesburg said that it was high time that Europeans learned to address educated 'Bantoe' as 'Meneer'—Mister. Mr. Kgoare was a good example of such an educated 'Bantoe', the paper said.

Professor E. Davis, head of the Department of English, had said to me good-humouredly, 'Don't allow it to go to your head.' I had studied English under him since 1947 when I was still an undergraduate. It did go to my head, but in a way I don't think my professor would have foreseen. Sylvester and Jenny threw a party for me at their suburban home. They invited a few European friends and I invited both European and non-white friends. We were unconsciously violating the so-called traditional way of life in South Africa. We ate, drank, and danced furiously and at any time during that night police might have come in and arrested us, the non-whites for 'trespassing' or for not having night special passes or for drinking so much as a tumbler of beer. And then Sylvester and Jenny might have been arrested for supplying so much as a tumbler of beer to Africans. But we had ceased to care: each one of us had at one time and another suffered worse humiliations. We taught our Indian friend, Barney Desai, a Sotho folk song and we stamped it out on the floor. That is how the M.A. degree went to my head. Going home that night we were stopped by five different batches of policemen over the distance of about fifteen miles: a ghastly reminder of motion pictures showing life in Germany and in occupied countries during the war. At every stop we were made to get out of our cars; we were searched, and we were asked to produce night passes, which we did not have. We lied our way through every batch and, frankly, the white constables were more conscientious than the Africans.

The M.A. degree knocked a little more pride into my head. A week later we had a party in our Orlando house and invited African, Coloured, Indian and European friends. This time it was for Sylvester, Jenny and other friends to violate the traditional way of life in South Africa. Jenny, an English-born woman, has the sort of pluck and cheek South African white snobbery cannot accommodate. Ten years in the country hadn't changed her a bit. Myrtle and Monty Berman, our other suburban friends, deserve the title 'foreign natives'. They are South African only by citizenship. They seem to be able to get over their social problems by laughing at the antics of white supremacy and throwing their energies into educational work among non-whites.

Other white friends who came were Jeanne and Malcolm. The rest were our African friends, forty of them teachers, nurses, clerks, doctors, messengers, journalists. About thirty stayed for the evening squeezed into 18 feet square of room in the dining-sitting-room, plus the 12 feet by 8 feet children's bedroom. Nobody seemed to mind the congestion. This time everything was on the *Drum* staff, 'instead of buying you a present', as Bloke Modisane, our debonair music writer, said.

Bloke had come in cowboy outfit. We got a secret little audience together for him to do a dramatic scene from the film, *The Fastest Gun Alive*. Gwigwi, the saxophonist and uncrowned king of comedy from Sophiatown, mimicked a European ex-boss of his and got our ribs almost splitting with laughter. There were the inevitable gate-crashers, among them a local woman with a large bosom, rather tipsy, who insisted on kissing me because 'you're so great, Zeke,' as she said. She was fond of playing younger than her reputed age of fifty.

We formed a ring and roared out a ranching song and drowned the music on the gramophone. Then we yelled out the *Imbube* chant and other African songs. We danced, ate and drank.

An African constable called to see what the occasion was. Someone gave him a glass of gin. He gulped it down, threw us a rapid smile and constable's salute and said it was all right, we could go on, and he would tell his colleagues that 'there was nothing wrong'. In normal circumstances all would have been wrong, in such a 'mixed' party.

Drum

At the beginning of 1957 the little imp in me whispered pesteringly: 'Budge, budge!' I was suddenly seized by a desire to leave South Africa for more sky to soar. I had been banned from teaching, and conditions were crushing me and I was shrivelling in the acid of my bitterness; I was suffocating. We were operating our house budget on a miserable income of £40 a month—*Drum* had raised my salary, but it had been pegged at that figure. I couldn't settle down to high-powered writing. I despaired often about the education of our children under the new system, but I felt I had no right to save them by taking them away, instead of fighting it out side by side with those whose children are also being brought up in a police state. And yet I felt I needed to build up moral and mental reserves. Arthur had told me about an Overseas Employment Bureau in London which was responsible for recruiting teachers for schools in East and West Africa, the Sudan and other countries. I applied and was sent a list of vacancies. I chose to teach in Lagos, Nigeria. A post was granted me in the C.M.S. Grammar School in Lagos, and in April I applied for a passport, with very little hope of being given it. Many 'harmless' Africans had been refused passports recently.

Interlude

Saturday night. Electric lights! How beautiful they look from a distance. So dull in themselves but, clustered like that, quivering, blinking, little fiery gems set in the fabric of night, they are fascinating. Standing here in a dark little world, viewing them from afar, miles away, you know they are beyond your reach. The more beautiful they look the more distant they appear —or, perhaps, the more distant they are the lovelier they look.

Here, a dark township, Orlando; below there, a seething mass of darkness with the usual Saturday night screams and groanings and drums: that's Shanty Town. Up there, another part of Orlando with lights, not too far to reach, but smiling and blinking at you ironically; then far away, clusters and clusters of them. They might have been bathed in water and emerged bright, clean, with a crystal texture, in the magical context of night. They look as if you might rake them into a container and leave a sieve on the surface of this summer night. They assume at once the man-made form and the unattainable, at any rate for the moment.

A hot, mothy night; there is no sleep. Out of the house into the yard. You take a deep breath and contemplate the beauty of distant electric lights until the children have gone to bed because you use the sitting-dining-room as a study. It has always been like this, since Second Avenue—waiting until the family has gone to bed before you did your studies. Rebecca has been at this sort of game too. It's the final year of her three-year diploma course in social work. She left teaching when Verwoerd, Minister of Native Affairs, made it clear that African teachers were going to be used for training children to be slaves. Day in and day out in the week she comes back from school at five o'clock and begins to cook, and I wash the children and studies begin at nine.

Your mate has gone to bed early tonight and there is a story you want to write—or rather you want to write a story and while you think how to begin you look at electric lights. You might try to place Parktown, or Parkwood, Emmarentia or Westcliff or Northcliff, where those lights can be; but you give it up after a while.

Pictures, fantasies, strivings, wishes, desires, memories and all other creatures of the intellect come to torment your being. Then you think how sordid life is; how ludicrous the very idea of life is; what a fruitless, petty, endless game it may be and mustn't be.

Things close in upon you; you find yourself in a tightly closed-up room. There seems no way out. You once flattered yourself that you had some talent, ability, honest thoughts and longings, and splendid ideals. You even fancied you had what man recognizes as ambition. Perhaps you had a trade or profession, and you wanted to tell the world what you wanted, what you felt and thought in some manner; you wanted to give life something the men would not allow you to—speak when you're spoken to, the world seemed to say. Eventually you didn't give life anything. It resented your efforts. The strivings and desires in you continued to torment you, to tease you out of yourself. But there was no exit from that prison. You knew it was your soul that was imprisoned.

Of course, the easiest way out would be to leave the soul in this cage, and start a new life, resolve to fling ambition to the winds, and just become a thoroughly sensuous animal; leave inspirations, ambition, ideals, planning and aesthetics to the elect. Or you might deny the existence of that in you which cherishes ambition and the rest, and seek no more than food, shelter, clothing. What joy and abundant satisfaction they must derive from life who did not wish for anything more than the bare necessities, like an ox! Or you might booze all these extra-physical stirrings out of your system, as so many, oh so many, educated Africans do.

Those electric lights in the distance continue to blink and tease the spirit of night: little sparkling fires, so unearthly, so inorganic.

But of course once you were sensitive to things that are, enough to know that they weren't there and should be, you couldn't go back, could you? And your tribal umbilical cord had long, oh so long, been severed and all the talk about Bantu culture and the Black man developing along his own lines was just so much tommy rot. You just felt the world getting too small for you, ever-contracting and shutting you in. A stuffy place, the world could become; as stuffy as the room from which you came out. If you tried to go away somewhere and ceased to care you'd still be in the larger denomination of the world which required man to care; you'd become a more bitter cynic; and while you shrivelled up in the acid of your cynicism the world wouldn't be at all worse off after your exit. No step backwards and so you must move and fight with the rest for a better and greater South Africa. Do it in some way but do it. It's no pastime but a desperate necessity and the knowing it galled you.

Orlando. A glorified Marabastad. Saturday night is the same as it was twenty-five years ago in Marabastad minus the ten-to-ten bell because now the curfew law is only for the city and suburbs to protect a frightened and neurotic white population which keeps revolvers and narcotic drugs under pillows. Yes, it is still the same, the only tarred roads being those leading to white superintendents' offices. The township has been spreading west and south since 1934 in three-roomed units; not east because that's the direction in which Johannesburg lies, twelve miles away; not north because that's where the line of gold mines is. We have been paying a sub-economic rental of fifty shillings a month for four rooms without electric lights or water-borne sewerage, and now the rents have gone up a scale stopping at £5. Near us is one of the biggest electric power stations in the world. As Orlando spreads into Meadowlands, Mofolo, Dube, Jabavu, Moroka, Molapo, Moletsane, holding more than 200,000 souls altogether, it also develops ulcers in the form of shanty towns; like the one just below us. And still the black metropolis grows, meeting other townships of refugees who have been removed from western towns which like Africans only as labourers. Faction fights must be a source of amusement to some white supreme chief of the Bantu who decided to force people into ethnic compartments and threw thousands of single men into huge dormitories in hostels with high fences around them.

There was a time when it was much better to be a tenant in a freehold township like Sophiatown than a municipal tenant, but the difference today is academic. Police continue to beat up and down the road in front of our house, not to protect human life and property but to look after the law and demand passes. Constant police patrols in the white man's areas have hurled the flame of violence to our doorsteps. Comparative cleanliness and bigness blunt the edge of political discontent here but you know you're in a ghetto and God, those lights are so far away, too far for you to reach. Between you and them is a pit of darkness, darkness charged with screams, groans, yells, cries, laughter and singing. They swell and reach a frantic pitch, only to be suppressed by the spirit of night.

From down here in the pit of sordidness, you hear humanity wailing for help, for food, for shelter; humanity gasping for air. And you know the scheme of things has come full circle: life thrown into a barbed-wire tangle; the longer it is made to stay there the more it is entangling itself and hurting itself; and the more it is hurting itself the more impotent it is becoming, and the more it is failing to save itself; so much the longer it will remain in the coils, degraded.

'What can you or anyone else do now or in any foreseeable future?' Sasha, your Jewish friend, asks you. That's five years ago now. 'Can't you seek a new little dominion elsewhere where you can sow your seed with some measure of confidence it'll grow into something worth while?' He looked at you with soft searching eyes. And you know you must answer.

'I don't know yet,' you say. 'I know nothing except that the noose will tighten soon. To go elsewhere might be a worse evil. There's the stoic inside me that tells me to stay, I repeat to myself what our sages have often said: what has no end is a miracle.'

'That's not realistic.'

'Damn it all, Sasha, it isn't, at any rate when you look at the immediate future.'

'A necessary addition.'

But you knew that even the immediate future was not so near: all was dim before you.

The lights quiver eternally. They have taken on an indifferent, impersonal, hard and cold sort of beauty. Only they and the night have something between them. And they gradually become a symbol.

'How long are you going to postpone it?' asks Sasha.

'I don't know. But right now I think it's a crime to bring children into a world with such a country.'

'H'm, in your melancholy mood again?'

'Not more than is naturally necessary.'

'It's bad enough for the world to deny you many things without your religious self-denials. At least the one thing the world cannot stop me from having is children.'

'Religion doesn't come into it,' you say testily.

'I mean religion in the sense that you're not really afraid of the responsibility children bring with them, you're a hard-working man.'

Yes, five years ago, when you were on the labour market, you thought it criminal to litter the earth with children who would go through the same spiritual, and perhaps physical, agonies that you were experiencing. Not now, you kept saying, not just yet; perhaps never.

By God, this is a hot night, the air doesn't seem to move at all. There is a cough from the bedroom. Rebecca is stirring. How strange! Five years ago, on a night like this, you were standing on your veranda, looking out into those quivering distant lights and you were thinking of what Sasha had said and then Rebecca coughed and stirred and came out to join you. After a time she pressed closer against you and said You know, I'm going to have a baby. A what? A baby, are you not happy? And Time passed, during which the wheel of reconciliation with yourself, with the ageless and inevitable, turned many revolutions. Then the world around seemed to widen. You thought of Sasha, good kind Sasha. Your ears became insensible to all outside you. Something thawed inside you; your blood coursed warmly in your veins; gradually it dawned on you that you were going to be father of a third child, the one thing you couldn't be denied and you felt awkwardly happy . . . Five years ago.

The lights quiver as brightly as ever, looking so clean, so jubilant, so fresh, teasing the primitive springs of life in you which in turn respond to that symbolic call of the lights coming across to you, wrapped in the mystery of night.

Every so often, your third-born, Motswiri, now four, sees the police take people down to the charge office and municipal police beat up a man or boy in the street just as you used to see them do years back in Marabastad. And now Motswiri clings to you tightly when he sees a constable walk up or down the road and says *Ntate*, is the policeman going to arrest me is he going to take you is he going to take mamma? You hold the frightened kid close to you and think of Second Avenue the long long great divide. Another time Motswiri comes to you with imitation handcuffs crudely made of wire and shouts Bring your hands here, where's your pass I'll teach you not to be naughty again. Now he wants a torch and a baton and a big broad belt and a badge, how agonizing! That passport, will it ever come or is it wrapped up in those electric lights? Trevor's words keep coming back to you that when you want a thing very badly you get it. You also remember that those lights are no figment of the brain. . . .

Your eldest child, Anthony, now ten, keeps telling you in the morning when you go to the shop, usually Sunday mornings, that you mustn't forget your pass. Because he has seen a long queue of men and boys on Sunday mornings being marched through the streets as the police collected more pass offenders before finally landing at the charge office. More agony.

Whatever happened you knew the story on the greatest treason trial in South Africa was your swan song for *Drum* and you must quit. That other story the electric lights distracted your mind from —well, for the moment, I must pretend to the role of Hopkins and play 'Time's eunuch'.

Twenty-Three

TICKET TO NIGERIA

For five months I waited and waited, only to be told that I couldn't have a passport. I went to see an African minister of the Dutch Reformed Church whom I had known over a number of years. I asked his advice. From then onwards I made several trips between Johannesburg and Pretoria. I learned from him the whole process prescribed for Africans when they apply for passports. I knew only the first and last stages. The Native Commissioner collects your application, together with three copies of each testimonial of character from some person of authority, and a letter from your wife or dependants saying they consent to your leaving; then you pay £100 security. He, in his own good time, sends all the papers to the Chief Native Commissioner more than a hundred miles away in Pietersburg. He in turn and in his own good time sends the papers to the Native Affairs Department in Pretoria together with a duplicate of the local Commissioner's recommendation. The Security Branch of the C.I.D. send an independent report to the Native Affairs Department, which in turn forwards all the documents to the Secretary for the Interior.

The clergyman went straight to the C.I.D. headquarters in Pretoria. The chief of the department whipped out his file on me. It told the whole story. Since 1950 when I became secretary of the provincial association of teachers; about my writings in the press, my speeches against Bantu education and one Government measure and another. During the years when I was walking the streets of Johannesburg I made a number of speeches at mass political rallies. Speeches which came hot from the anvil, speeches spitting vitriol. All these had been recorded. I knew they had been, and secretly I knew why the application for a passport had been rejected.

When a man's record screams against him like this, the C.I.D. chief was in effect saying to the pastor, how can we let him out of the country? But if I wasn't let out, the pastor argued, I'd become more and more bitter and turn Communist. The Chief said, 'Call him to my office and let's hear what he has to say.'

I went, prepared to see the whole thing through. I'm still wondering what the Chief wants in a Security Branch of that most dreaded and unpopular institution in South Africa. In place of the tough, rough, skittish and callous type that the ordinary police often are, I was face to face with a cultured white man. Paternal, yes, but human and soft-spoken. That policeman who always made my hair bristle was not there. The Chief wanted to know if I could speak Afrikaans, his language. From that moment we never spoke a word of English. He asked me to tell him my life history. In the course of it all, he expressed surprise at my fluency. I didn't feel flattered. He took down notes on the subjects I had done for my degrees; on the whites I had been associated with at various times; he wanted to know how I had come by the post in Nigeria, who had helped me to secure it, who my referees were. I didn't tell him all, I'm sure he knew.

He said after it all that he could appreciate why I had felt so bitter after I had been banned from teaching; that the Government wasn't really intending to oppress us, as we thought; that he himself had served under the United Party Government; that in fact he personally was all for the Black man's progress, and that he was the one man who had urged the Government to allow Africans to buy European liquor, even in the face of opposition from his church, the Dutch Reformed. 'If the last thing I can ever do in my life,' he said, 'is to save you from Communism, I'll do it.' So he'd ask the Secretary for the Interior to let me out to Nigeria. But if ever I should find it necessary to speak publicly about South Africa, said the Chief, it would not do to speak ill about the country that had given me the education I had. I was to bear in mind the fact that South Africa was doing more for its non-white population than any colonial power in Africa. He wasn't going to ask me to promise anything, he said. I had the pastor to thank for his kind offices. Within the next two weeks I should get my passport.

This interview took place three weeks before my tentative plane booking for September 6th. Those three weeks I lurked in the corridors of Union Buildings. Every time I went I was told by some junior clerk who writes out passports that my documents and the C.I.D. chief's latest letter were on the desk of the Secretary of the Interior awaiting his endorsement. During those weeks I simply felt the beating of the great wings of official power, ridden either with indifference or positive hate. There were no harsh words like those Pass or Post Office clerks use. Here, show of power was deliberate, sure and silently arrogant, like the pillars and walls and foundations of Union Buildings. The pastor accompanied me every time I went, and it was always through him that word was passed on to me. '*Die groot baas is nog besig*—the big boss is still busy,' the clerk kept saying. The pastor struck me as having had years of training in patience. I was both amazed and alarmed at my own capacity for waiting. I had always dreaded the day I should find it easy to wait or to accept a situation. I was really alarmed, even as I was floating in the no-time of waiting and thinking and feeling. I could pay untold gold to know just what the 'big boss' was busy at. And still the wings of the giant bird of power continued to beat about me. The feel of it hurt deep, but somehow I held on. The day before I took the plane to Lagos, I went to Pretoria to fetch the passport.

On September 6th I said good-bye to my friends, to South Africa. What I had wished and dreamt for about ten months were crowded into those few moments as the KLM plane took the clouds. What a day in thirty-seven years of a man's life!

Rebecca and our three children, Anthony, Theresa and Motswiri, joined me on December 22nd. She had been subjected to the same humiliations as I had been, minus a paternal lecture, and been given her passport on the eve of her departure, wrongly filled in. The morning of the day she left she had to go back to the immigration office to have the passport corrected and the plane had to be delayed an hour because of it.

The C.M.S. Grammar School paid all our single fares. My friends, Arthur and Trevor and the lady who used to help us in dramatics and has been a constant pillar of support to my family, gave us continuous encouragement and material help in our new venture.

Many of my friends tried to dissuade me from leaving. 'Stay on in the struggle,' they kept saying. 'I'm contributing nothing,' I told them. 'I can't teach and I want to teach, I can't write here and I want to write.'

'You've got all the material you want here, and the spur is always there.'

'That's the trouble: it's a paralysing spur; you must keep moving, writing at white heat, everything full of vitriol; hardly a moment to think of human beings as human beings and not as victims of political circumstance. But one must crack up somewhere. Maybe this is it for me. I'm sick of protest creative writing and our South African situation has become a terrible cliché as literary material. It's just been a continuous battle to feed and clothe a family amid the yells of mad white men who are doing all to stop me and sap my energy so that I've nothing left for writing.'

'Want comfort?'

'A reasonable amount.' Even so, I didn't think I was making myself clear about what exactly I wanted. I did, however, feel the burning need to replenish mental and moral reserves. And then there was the education of the children. Maybe it would be a temporary break, I didn't know. It would mean leaving behind persons and institutions that had played such a vital part in the shaping of my life, some to the good, others to the bad.

My paternal grandmother in Pietersburg, I hear, is very old and grey. My father died not long after my mother, but not before his second wife had left him for another man, left him with three children. I don't know where his two sisters are. My younger brother is happily married and has seven children. He was a clerk in the Department of Native Affairs for several years, and he's now looking for another job, having left government service.

Our sister's marriage ended on the rocks. She had to divorce her husband after he had given her five children; divorced him in circumstances that smelled terribly of paraffin from a burning pressure stove and boiling meat and potatoes and curry . . . I can't bear to think of it. She is a machinist in a clothing factory in Johannesburg, and barely manages to maintain herself and the children. But according to the new labour regulations, her job must now become the preserve of the white worker. Her former husband has succeeded in persuading the Orlando superintendent to drive her and the children out of their house and they have gone to one of the shanty towns sixteen miles out of Johannesburg.

Grandmother from Second Avenue is now eighty and sickly. After changing domicile with Aunt Dora and her sons, she is now living with her youngest in the freehold township of Lady Selborne, Pretoria. Like Sophiatown, the township must move because it is a 'black spot'—too near whites—and wherever the residents go they will not be allowed to own land. Grandmother still prays every morning and evening and she manages to go to church on Sundays and Thursday afternoons for the women's prayer meeting. But her son and daughter-in-law have to leave for work at four in the morning because they are about nine miles out of town; so she kneels alone to pray. She hobbles with a stick as she dusts the furniture and collects pots and dishes for washing up. Aunt Dora has five children now. She is much steadier since she came to live in Lady Selborne. Somehow her dignity makes me identify her with my mother, and I love her. Her husband is still working at the State Museum in town, but he has thinned down from tuberculosis. They also will have to move soon, just when they intended to mortgage their property in order to put up a decent building on it with living-rooms and rooms to let. Their eldest son is a teacher, one son is doing matriculation in a day school, and two daughters are working in town, without a profession or trade. Rebecca's mother, over sixty now, is in the section of Sophiatown which is the next to be bulldozed. She has a house with tenants in another street farther on, which house she had put up after bending the other property. What compensation she does get will all go to cover the twelve hundred pounds she owes the building society.

Zeph Mothopeng is an articled clerk in a lawyer's office in Johannesburg, and is expected to complete soon. Isaac Matlare has completed his law studies and is now a solicitor. Zeph's second-born lost his sight after our dismissal, and is at the Athlone School for the Blind near Cape Town; the school Arthur Blaxall and his wife founded in the 1920's. It has been a rough time for Zeph and his wife, a schoolmistress. For the same reason that Rebecca left teaching to study social work, Zeph's wife has also done so. In addition to maintaining three other grown-up children, they have a son in secondary day school. Zeph is one of the small band of persons inside the ANC called Africanists, who say Africans should dissolve their alliance with the other racial groups. The reasons they give are that the minority groups don't really feel the white man's oppression in the way Africans do; that an alliance with these groups clouds the clear-cut issue of African nationalism and the Africa-for-the-Africans slogan; that the African is quite capable of winning freedom without the interference of the other races; that the Freedom Charter of the Congress of the People is a crazy document which wants the land shared equally among all South Africans. 'How can I share the land equally with Strijdom and his crowd,' says Zeph, 'when his forefathers and compatriots stole it from us?'

Isaac is a member of the Unity Movement. He's a short, brilliant fellow. A bitter cynic with a sharp stinging tongue for his political enemies, Congressites included. When he wears a dirty frown over one eye, then it means that he has been spitting venom. His wife is a nurse.

Thinking back to the years at Ezenzeleni, I'm reminded of Adam Daniels, the orphaned, blind Coloured man whom I used to teach typewriting. He plays the saxophone less now, because he is up to his neck in politics. He is Transvaal chairman of the Coloured People's Organization, one of the ANC's allies.

Arthur and Florence Blaxall have long left Ezenzeleni. Arthur is organizing secretary of the Christian Council of South Africa. To think of them is to remember Ezenzeleni: Arthur walking with a drooping shoulder because he had lost a lung in World War I; Arthur, packing his bag to prepare for a long journey by train or car or plane to attend a meeting or to see some Government official about blind welfare work or about a school for African deaf-mutes; Mrs. Blaxall taking long strides up the road past Ezenzeleni offices, towards Palmer Hostel, the eye hospital and clinic where she was superintendent. I always think of her patiently going through the daily routine of teaching the deaf, dumb and blind Radcliffe to express himself; a boy she had adopted when he was moving on all fours because of spinal meningitis and trained to walk straight.

I remember how I disliked Arthur Blaxall's impetuosity and impatience towards folk of lesser intellect than his. But I admired him for his genuine desire to understand the social, political, economic and other problems that harass the non-European. He was always probing young minds and holding his ear to the ground to know other people's sufferings and seek a way to help. He has always attended political and trade union meetings, learning patiently, but never condescending or imposing himself. Now that my religious outlook has changed, I think of him as an enigma. It continues to puzzle me how a man like him, unorthodox in his denominational allegiance and missionary outlook, maintains steadfast Christian-pacifist convictions in situations where the very forces of oppression he does not like have thrown all ethics to the winds. We disagree on many points of political and religious practice, but the picture that comes to my mind of him is always that of the unmissionary missionary.

Twenty years ago I was caned by the then headmaster of St. Peter's Secondary School for having sworn at white cyclists. He said we were unwittingly inviting Rosettenville to root out St. Peter's. In 1956 the school closed down by Government decree. Ironically, not because a Black boy insulted a white man, although Rosettenville whites are just as responsible for the school's removal as the governments that represents their interests. St.

Peter's was moved because it dared give a decent education to non-white in 'an area preserved for whites'—in every literal and figurative sense of the phrase.

It has done a good bit. Many of those heroes and heroines who chalked riders all over the blackboards have made good. They are lawyers, doctors, university lecturers, nurses, teachers, social workers. A number of these are political leaders. Among these unsung heroes are: Joseph Mokoena, M.Sc., now lecturing in mathematics in Kumasi, Ghana; Ambrose Phahle, M.Sc., lecturing in physics at Fort Hare University College; Margaret Chuene, medical doctor on the Rand; Dinchu Tavaria, medical doctor on the Rand; Aaron Lebona, now a medical practitioner in the Free State; Samuel Senokoanyane, a medical doctor in Johannesburg; Oliver Tambo, B.Sc., now an attorney in Johannesburg and general secretary of ANC. Some of those who followed were to find themselves caught up in the political struggle of their people, and arrested on charges of treason; Jo Matthews, attorney; Henry Makgothi, teacher; Alfred Hutchinson, teacher and writer; Joe Molefi, business man, and Advocate Duma Nokwe. All these and others went out of St. Peter's gates with a matriculation certificate. They scrounged and mouched around for bursaries to proceed to Fort Hare. Some were lucky enough to find sponsors among big-hearted Europeans. Some were flung willy-nilly into the brutal South African labour market on the gates of which may be imagined the inscription 'MESSENGERS ONLY'. Once a messenger, always a messenger; if not a messenger, a teacher or nothing else. Court interpreter, police sergeant or machinist are all levelled by the title of 'messenger'. Some of the girls who left St. Agnes's went to medical school, most of them took up nursing and teaching.

The celebration of Adams College centenary in 1955 was her swan song. It came under the guillotine of the Bantu Education Act when the Native Affairs Department commandeered all African schools and made it virtually impossible for any person or group of persons to run a private school. The Adams board of governors intended to do this, but the conditions were unworkable. The college has closed down. Kilnerton Institution has been ordered to go because the Group Areas Act has decided that it is in a 'white area'.

The Syndicate of African Artists has folded up now. Money. The Government kept telling us that if we wanted their help we would have to restrict our membership to Africans and stop organizing multi-racial audiences. We enjoyed every step of that run of nine years: those delightful intimate evenings of music and drama. At the Bach and Mozart evenings we had Father Martin Jarrett-Kerr, C.R. playing the clarinet and Father Trelawney Ross, C.R. at the piano. Both of them came from St. Peter's Priory, Rosettenville. And then they have a trio with Khabi Mngoma, tenor. Martin is a small priest with a brilliant intellect and abundant vitality. His special field is among African nurses and he has thrown himself into the nurses' struggle against apartheid in their profession. He is generally considered to have put on Father Trevor Huddleston's mantle in non-European politics. The Baragwanath Non-European Hospital kicked him out of its board because they thought he was being a nuisance standing up for the rights of nurses. Apart from being a notable literary critic, he is a musician.

Khabi Mngoma possesses music certificates of the University of South Africa both in theory and performance. He has failed to get an overseas training, and alas, frustration will drive him into the anonymous group of singers who are 'called upon to give us an item' at birthday parties. He is music organizer employed by the non-European department of the city council.

Before the curtain came down on us, we were able to see Emlyn Williams in a Dylan Thomas recital at the Social Centre in the city. He sent us through the roof. Sylvester Stein wangled an engagement from Sir Lewis Casson and Dame Sybil Thorndyke who were then visiting South Africa. We organized a good multiracial audience. It was a most moving experience to watch that wonderful pair in action, doing scenes from *Macbeth*. The bleak bareness of the stage disappeared in an instant. All one was conscious of was the magnificent moment when actor and poetry were no more two entities but one glorious sweeping experience. By way of thanks, I recited Chekov's monologue, *On the Harmfulness of Tobacco*. I was highly flattered by the enthusiastic applause and a special word of congratulations from Sir Lewis and Dame Sybil.

Epilogue

I can never summon enough courage to read a line from any of the stories that were published in 1947 under the title, *Man Must Live* again. In ten years my perspective has changed enormously from escapist writing to protest writing and, I hope, to something of a higher order, which is the ironic meeting between protest and acceptance in their widest terms. Maybe from the chaff I have been writing since 1947 a few grains have emerged. One story, *The Suitcase*, appeared in *New World Writing*, a New York anthology of prose and poetry, in 1955. The story was recommended to the publishers by Nadine Gordimer, who had already made a name as a novelist and short-story writer. The story was later translated into Dutch for an anthology of negro stories. It is in essence a true story, told to me by Rebecca about an incident that had occured in Sophiatown.

No South African journals circulating mainly among whites would touch any of my stories, nor any others written by a non-white, unless he tried to write like a European and adopted a European name. Two or three Coloured writers told me once that they had slipped through the readers' sieve and become immortalized in European pulp. But I have been too busy fighting my own bitterness without trying to prostitute myself in that fashion. Some articles of mine, however, have appeared in the readers' columns in the white press. Then obviously the particular paper was not committed. Very rarely do articles written by non-whites appear in the white press. Every time something has been published that I wrote, I have felt patronized. But then always I wrote because something burned inside me beyond bearing; the desire to correct some stupidly over-enthusiastic cabinet minister or some smug suburban white person who, as grandmother would say, pretends not to know which side of the body the

African's heart sits. Moreover, there is only one independent paper run by a Coloured group in Cape Town, *Torch*; independent in the sense that it is not managed by whites. It has no readers' columns, and one has to sympathize with Unity Movement or All-African Convention ideology to write for it. The only one left with a multi-racial editorial board is *New Age*. But it is hardly enough for increasing non-white readership in a country where literacy among non-whites is higher than anywhere else on the Continent. And then *New Age* is always in financial straits.

As soon as I landed in Nigeria in September 1957 and settled into school work, I wrote and finished the second half of this book. Immediately I felt the difference between writing here and in a South African social climate. Somehow it feels like having just climbed down from a vehicle that has been rocking violently for countless miles. I am able to write articles on Nigeria in-between times, but I haven't settled down to a short story yet. I have been trying to sniff around and find a distinctive smell to guide me. It has been eluding me. I now realize what a crushing cliché the South African situation can be as literary material.

I admire the white man's achievements, his mind that plans tall buildings, powerful machinery. I used to want to justify myself and my own kind to the white man. I later discovered that it wasn't worth it. It was to myself and to my kind I needed to justify myself. I think now the white man has no right to tell me how to order my life as a social being, or order it for me. He may teach me how to make a shirt or to read and to write, but my forebears and I could teach him a thing or two if only he would listen and allow himself time to feel. Africa is no more for the white man who comes here to teach and to control her human and material forces and not to learn.

Countless times I have dreamt about the deep valleys and craggy mountains of Pietersburg. I have revisited them in my dreams, never in flesh. Every time I have been trapped by the huge mountains and I have heard endless echoes chasing after me, chasing, while I ran all the time, ran into a dawn of sirens and motor-car hooters and bicycle bells and trolley carts and . . . breakfasts.

I admire that man who, like Bach in his music, can make definite statements of religious faith. Yet I'm impatient of Robert Browning's bloated, blustering certitudes about God. Reminds me: my life up to now has been a series of events through which it seems I was driven by some sort of inevitability. Yes, I've thought, and planned and suffocated and had my share of hate and felt cloyed, no more than my fellow-African, but I've always been hurled back into the furnace of reality and I couldn't decide one way or another. And then, it seems, some big wave came and carried me along with it to the inevitable shore, and then I knew I must be doing the right thing. I've felt the heartburn of frustration and didn't feel sorry for my hates. I can't feel sorry even now, removed as I am from it all. The other man shut me off in Second Avenue. And now he has taught me never to expect mercy—but who wants mercy? Never to beg for favours through the kitchen door, but to take by force what I possess while he wasn't looking. He has driven me against the wall so that I never forget I am black. He has taught me to lie to him and feel triumphant. Because he has made me get used to the back door I have bought goods, stolen from his shop by his own Black worker, for less than the cost. And there are millions of me. We know almost everything about him and he knows nothing about us, so we still hold the trump card.

It is the lingering melody of a song that moves me more than the initial experience itself; it is the lingering pain of a past insult that rankles and hurts me more than the insult itself. Too dumb to tell you how immensely this music or that play or this film moves me, I wait for the memory of the event.

All my life people have been at my soul, tugging at it in different directions. I have chafed under unrelenting controls, enthusiastic evangelizing, ruthless police watchfulness. So many other hands have been reaching out for me, and so many voices have been babbling about my ears like the idiotic rattling of wheels of a moving train and I must scream, *leave me alone*. Downright anarchy, downright individualism, you may say. I enjoy a fair amount of both, at any rate in my thought-life. This Nigerian sun will burn up at least such prejudice and bitterness and hate of thirty-seven years as haven't grown into my system like kikuyu grass. That may amount to very little. But there will always be that smouldering anger against poverty, injustice and the legalized bullying of the small man by the strong one.

I am sitting in the spacious garden of a Lagos house as I write this epilogue, and it is early January, the heat is much drier than when I came here. Before deciding to write I set on a recording of Vivaldi's *Four Seasons*. As the music floats across to me from the sitting-room, I remember a beautiful winter morning in Nadine Gordimer's big garden in Parktown, Johannesburg. Nadine, Anthony, who had come down from London to collect material for a book, and I were listening to Vivaldi in the same fashion. 'I find Vivaldi most satisfying,' Nadine said. Yes, after Beethoven's roaring furnaces, Mozart's sweet, sad, delicate humour, Schubert's lyrical sweetness, Chopin's melancholy nostalgia, after Tchaikowsky's capricious moods, Bach's overwhelming bigness and after Rimsky-Korsakoff's enchantment, it is a cool and refreshing experience to come back to Vivaldi.

Yes, basking in this Nigerian heat, I feel cool inside me. I stretch myself like the lizards there on the warm concrete wall. I have brought with me prejudices and anger to a country where they are almost altogether alien now. I'm breathing the new air of freedom, and now the barrel of gall has no bottom any more. I shall soon know what to do with this freedom. For the moment, I'm still baffled, and my canoe still feels the momentum that launched it in Second Avenue. But what a glorious sense of release!

Epilogue

There is complacency here. Often, I think, too much of it. The secondary schoolboys I'm handling and the South African high schoolboy are worlds apart. In the south the boys and I were caught up in a violent situation. We both carried a pass and we could be stopped any time by the police and searched or arrested the moment we stepped out of the school grounds. We were both hungering for many things and getting little, which in turn sharpened the edge of our longings. I responded to every throb of pain and restlessness in them, and I think they responded to my yearnings. Here, the atmosphere is placid. In a sense there is a vacuum. But oh, what a sense of release. And what a glorious opportunity for Rebecca and me to replenish our moral and mental reserves. The children are very happy, and they will be able to learn something worth while, something that is fit for all mankind, not for slaves.

The church as an ecumenical force in South Africa has been on the retreat since before Union in 1910. And then the Church, with its emphasis on the value of the individual personality, has continued stubbornly to bring outmoded standards to the situation; a situation where a powerful *herrenvolk* has for three centuries done everything in the interests of the *volk*.

Where persons have been oppressed as a race group, the Church has sought safeguards and concessions for the individual, evading the necessity and responsibility of group action. And while it fixed its gaze on Calvary or kept up an aloofness from political realities, the road has been slipping back under its feet. It never seems to have occurred to the Church that right under its nose has been growing a calculating white barbarism, among those it considered as hereditary custodians of Christianity, custodians who need mission stations in their very midst. I cannot but reaffirm what I said in a B.B.C. talk in 1955 on the African intellectual: that to us, the Church has become a symbol of the dishonesty of the West. I'm still suspending belief and disbelief as far as the necessity or uselessness of organized religion goes. All I know is that I found no use for it in South Africa; that since 1947 when I stopped going to church, I have become progressively weary of all the trappings of mystical formalism that go together with South African 'churchianity'. For the moment, I'm content to move on, free of this sort of allegiance, exposing myself to the impacts of as many ways of life as possible. I'm glad that I can at last exercise that right.